Women Resisting Violence

Praise for this book

This highly accessible book is concerned with one of the most important issues in Latin America today and in the future – violence against women. Its uniqueness relates to its focus on women's resistance to violence, rather than women as victims of violence. In a context where diversity is key, it emphasizes the intersectional dimensions of women's experiences. The text is accompanied by useful boxes, figures and podcast links. Women Resisting Violence will be core reading for policy-makers, researchers and students alike.

Caroline Moser, Emeritus Professor, University of Manchester;
Honorary Professor, UCL

Latinoamérica es el continente con mayores índices de VAWG pero, a su vez, con un tremendo potencia de múltiples resistencias. Este libro demuestra una vez más la importancia de los lazos de sororidad entre feministas de la academia e indígenas feministas proponiendo creativas formas de resistencia y teorizando desde el sur. Como dice la canción: nos sembraron miedo, nos crecieron alas...

Latin America is the continent with the highest rates of VAWG but, at the same time, with a tremendous power of multiple resistances. This book demonstrates, once again, the significance of the bonds of sisterhood between academic feminists and indigenous feminists proposing creative forms of resistance and theorizing from the South. As the song says: "they sowed fear in us, we grew wings..."

Rocío Silva Santisteban, Peruvian poet, feminist activist, scholar,
and former member of Congress

Women Resisting Violence is a unique exploration of the different ways that women are resisting gendered violence. The book uses a powerful combination of different resistance strategies across a range of contexts. It provides an excellent insight into gender and intersectionality including an analysis of the impact of VAWG on women in all their diversity and fascinating examples of the different ways in which VAWG has disproportionate impacts on Indigenous women, Black women, women from urban and rural locations, migrants, and persons from LGBTQ+ groups.

Dr Erika McAslan Fraser, Ending Violence against
Women and Children Helpdesk

The alarming rates of violence against women in Latin America can leave one feeling overwhelmed and hopeless. But by highlighting concrete, effective strategies and actions–led by those most affected by this violence-, the book Women Resisting Violence plays a critical role in finding solutions. It's a valuable resource for activists, journalists and researchers, and a powerful record of grassroots resistance.

Silvia Viñas, Executive Producer and co-host of El hilo weekly news podcast from Radio Ambulante Estudios and VICE News.

The struggle of Latin American organizations to combat gender-based violence is a heroic story. This book is a superb summary of grassroots efforts and is key to understanding how to take the ideals of equality and convert them into policy and action. An excellent read that allows you to learn about the difficulties, passion and experiences of thousands of activists in Latin America. Wherever you might live, study or practice, many of these challenges will also resonate with your own.

Pamela Zaballa, CEO at NO MORE.

'The state doesn't protect me, my friends do.' This book shows very comprehensively how this slogan chanted by Latin American women in protests across the continent is put into practice. From cities, to rural areas, in homes, intimate spaces and even through their own bodies, we see how women who are neglected by the state get together to protect each other from different types of intersectional gendered violence.

Their actions include mass pro-choice and anti-femicide mobilizations, protecting indigenous lands and nature, using art to fight for social change, creating women's houses and apps to make cities safer, and campaigning for migrants and domestic workers. These are acts of resistance with which women confront systemic violence and create a better and safer world for us all – something that's especially important due to the increased inequalities caused by COVID-19.

We should all read this book to remember how strong the enemy is and to join the fight from our own position and possibilities (wherever we may be and to the best of our abilities). As we read here, everything counts, even waiting to receive a message when your friend gets home.

Catalina May, Las Raras podcast

Women Resisting Violence
Voices and Experiences from Latin America

Women Resisting Violence Collective

Published by Practical Action Publishing Ltd
and Latin America Bureau

Practical Action Publishing Ltd
25 Albert Street Rugby,Warwickshire, CV21 2SD, UK
www.practicalactionpublishing.com

Latin America Bureau (Research & Action) Ltd
Enfield House, Castle Street, Clun, Shropshire, SY7 8JU, UK
www.lab.org.uk

ISBN 978-1-90901-486-2 Paperback
ISBN 978-1-90901-491-6 Hardback
ISBN 978-1-90901-480-0 Electronic PDF

Women Resisting Violence Collective (2022) *Women Resisting Violence: Voices and Experiences from Latin America*, Rugby, UK: Practical Action Publishing
<http://dx.doi.org/10.3362/9781909014800>.

Since 1974, Practical Action Publishing has published and disseminated books and information in support of international development work throughout the world. Practical Action Publishing is a trading name of Practical Action Publishing Ltd (Company Reg. No. 1159018), the wholly owned publishing company of Practical Action. Practical Action Publishing trades only in support of its parent charity objectives and any profits are covenanted back to Practical Action (Charity Reg. No. 247257, Group VAT Registration No. 880 9924 76).

Latin America Bureau (Research and Action) Limited is a UK registered charity (no. 1113039). Since 1977 LAB has been publishing books, news, analysis and information about Latin America, reporting consistently from the perspective of the region's poor, oppressed or marginalized communities, and social movements. In 2015 LAB entered into a publishing partnership with Practical Action Publishing.

The views and opinions in this publication are those of the author and do not represent those of Practical Action Publishing Ltd or its parent charity Practical Action, nor those of Latin America Bureau. Reasonable efforts have been made to publish reliable data and information, but the authors and publishers cannot assume responsibility for the validity of all materials or for the consequences of their use.

The authors and the publishers have used their best efforts to secure permissions for the use of all text and images in this book.

A catalogue record for this book is available from the British Library.

Cover image by: Liliana Adaluz Romera Seguro @lilophilia
https://lilophilia.com/
Typeset by JMR Digital

Contents

Figures, boxes, and table

Figures

Boxes

Table

About the Women Resisting Violence Collective

The WRV Collective reflects the feminist and collaborative decision-making processes underpinning the project and the writing of this book. This book has emerged from two projects on gendered and intersectional violence; collective efforts that have entailed a range of activities and which capture multiple initiatives and inputs. The creation of the Women Resisting Violence (WRV) website, blog, and podcast have been central to the work of the WRV Collective.

Jelke Boesten is a professor of Gender and Development at the Department of International Development, King's College London. She writes about gender-based violence in war and peace, post conflict justice, and memory and the arts in Latin America, with particular focus on Peru.

Andrea Espinoza is a feminist researcher focused on women's and Indigenous people's rights in Latin America, particularly in Ecuador and the Andean region. She is a postdoctoral fellow at University of Exeter, with a project enquiring how socialism shapes sexual and reproductive health rights in Latin America, particularly in Ecuador and Peru. Her PhD thesis looked at Indigenous women's paths through violence in plurilegal Ecuador.

Cathy McIlwaine is a professor of Geography at King's College London. Her research focuses on issues of gender, poverty, and violence in cities of the global South, and on migration and gendered violence among the Latin American community in London. She works collaboratively with a range of organizations and artists in Brazil and London.

Louise Morris is a journalist and audio producer who's made podcasts, radio, and audiobooks for BBC Radio 4, NPR, Audible, Pottermore, and the BBC World Service. Louise produced the Women Resisting Violence podcast and wrote the chapters Fighting Machismo: Women on the Front Line; and Cultural Resistance for LAB's *Voices of Latin America* book.

Patricia Muñoz Cabrera (PhD) is an international research consultant and trainer on gender and intersectionality in development policies. Her postdoctoral research in sociology (U. of Sao Paulo, Brazi) focused on intersectional analysis of public policies in Argentina, Brazil, and Chile. She has worked for European and international institutions, NGOs, and grassroots organizations. She was Chair of the former WIDE Network and is a member of the working group on feminist economic literacy at WIDE+. Her current research work focuses on the political economy of intersectional violence.

Moniza Rizzini Ansari is a postdoctoral research fellow at the Federal University of Rio de Janeiro, School of Law. She holds a PhD in Law from Birkbeck, University of London and previously worked as a research associate at King's College London, Department of Geography. Her research focuses on the legal geography of poverty and violence in urban margins in Rio de Janeiro, Brazil.

Marilyn Thomson is an independent gender consultant working on issues such as the rights of migrant and refugee women, violence against women and girls, and the care economy. She lived and worked in Latin America for many years carrying out research and projects with universities, international NGOs, and grassroots women's organizations, including a domestic workers organization in Mexico. Her PhD thesis focused on the politics of domestic service. She was co-director of the UK-based Central America Women's Network (which ran from 1992-2017).

Rebecca Wilson is Managing Editor at Latin America Bureau. As a journalist, she has worked with El Tiempo in Colombia and written about Latin American politics and culture for LAB, NACLA, Sounds and Colours, Barbican Centre, and BristoLatino - where she was Editor-in-Chief. She has also worked as a research assistant in the Department of Hispanic, Portuguese and Latin American Studies at University of Bristol and volunteers with FLAWA (London's Festival of Latin American Women in Arts).

Acknowledgements

The Women Resisting Violence project was funded by the ESRC Impact Acceleration Account (IAA) held at King's College London for a project entitled 'Women Resisting Gendered and Intersectional Violence: developing a podcast audio series to share "best practice" and influence policymaking', as part of a policy and practice fellowship between King's College London (Cathy McIlwaine and Jelke Boesten) and the Latin America Bureau, and for which we are grateful. It received additional support from the National Lottery Community Fund. We are grateful to the Latin America Bureau Council and especially Mike Gatehouse as well as Niall Sreenan at the Policy Institute at King's College London for facilitating this funding.

We would also like to thank the following contributors, interviewees and volunteers whose inputs have been essential for the creation of the book:

Ana Laura Aquino, Marcelina Bautista, Mary Goldsmith (interviewed for Chapter 2); Veronica Gago (Chapter 3); Jessica Acuña, Clara Merino (Chapter 4); Melissa Munz (Chapter 5); Natalia Iguiñiz (Chapter 6).

A series of blogs were commissioned for the WRV website. We are grateful to the following people who contributed to these (in addition to WRV Collective members):

Eva Alterman Blay, Fernanda Alvarez Piñeiro, Max Drabwell McIlwaine, Claudia Hasanbegovic, Elizabeth Jiménez-Yañez, Tallulah Lines, Rosie Thornton, Natasha Tinsley, Stephanie Wallace, Alice Wright.

The podcast involved the following who we would like to thank (in addition to the WRV Collective members):

Jennifer Alexander, Claudia Alves, Stef Arreaga, Ella Barnes, Theodora Bradford, Carolina Cal Angrisani, Serena Assumpção, Alma Carballo, Vianney Claret Hernandez Mejia, Ameno Cordóva, Eliane Correa, Cecilia Cruz, Morgan Fairless Brown, Michele Gandra, Gil Garcia, Mayra Jimenez, Elizabeth Jimenez-Yañez, Najlla Kay, Rebeca Lane, Julia Leal, Quimy de León, Esmeralda Lobos, Luciana Lopes, Gilberto Martins, Larisa Muñoz, Giselle Nirenberg, Jonathan Panta, Renata Peppl, Juliana Postico, Hebe Powell, Noelle Resende, Mariana

Reyes, Cristina Reynoso López, Moniza Rizzini Ansari, Rafael Rocha, Ana Lucía Rojas, Eliana Sousa Silva, Natasha Tinsley, Uppbeat, and WARA (see Appendix for more details).

The research discussed in Chapter 5 on migration was funded by the ESRC (ES/N013247/1), the ESRC Impact Acceleration Account (IAA) held at King's College London, and by the Latin American Women's Rights Service and the Lloyd's Foundation. The research on which Chapter 1 on gendered urban violence was drawn from was funded by the ESRC (ES/N013247/1) and the British Academy and the Global Challenges Research Fund (HDV190030). These projects were conducted with a range of partners including the Department of Geography at King's College London, Latin American Women's Rights Service, People's Palace Projects, Queen Mary University of London, Redes da Maré, the Federal University of Rio de Janeiro, Migrants in Action, Museu da Pessoa, and CASA Latin American Theatre Festival.

Thanks to LAB's Friend of LAB Patrons for their support:

Jon Barnes, Alistair Clark, Malcolm Coad, Ivette Hernandez, Elizabeth Lethbridge, Mandy Macdonald, Sophie Muir, Nick Parker, David Raby, Bert Schouwenburg, Rachel Sieder, David Treece.

Introduction

'We are weaving collective knowledge in order to transform unjust policies and practices.' (Clara Merino, Luna Creciente Foundation, Ecuador)

Marilyn Thomson & Patricia Muñoz Cabrera

Latin America has one of the highest rates of gender-based violence and femicide in the world, an incidence which dramatically increased and intensified during the COVID-19 pandemic. While there is much research on the nature and causes of such violence, there is little exploration of the courageous projects designed to address it. Foregrounding the voices of those affected and those transforming their communities, in order to learn from their innovative responses, is the key aim behind our collective project Women Resisting Violence.

The introduction provides a brief overview of the panorama of gendered and intersectional violence against Latin American women and girls, and the types of strategies women are putting in place to resist and mitigate it.

Background to the book

This book, written collaboratively by the WRV Collective, builds on key findings from two projects implemented since 2006. The first is a collaboration between King's College London and the Latin American Bureau, Women Resisting Gendered and Intersectional Violence (2021-2022). The project documents some of the innovative ways in which Latin American women have addressed and tried to mitigate violence against women and girls (VAWG), showcased through a website and blog, a narrative podcast,[1] public events, and this book. One of our main aims was to foreground the voices of Latin American women affected by VAWG in Latin America and among the diaspora residing beyond the continent, with a specific focus on the UK. We also highlighted the power of collaborations between civil society organizations and academic research projects.

One of the key findings is the way in which women have emerged as protagonists in challenging gendered violence, through developing innovative forms of resistance, resilience, and new proposals for trans-formation. These range from grassroots political responses, campaigns, and public protest to artistic engagements and community livelihood projects. We also found that VAWG remains deeply intersectional in its disproportionate impact on poor women in all their diversity (Black, Indigenous, from urban and rural locations, persons from LGTBQ+ groups, and migrants). And finally, we found that VAWG is embedded in wider forms of structural violence, especially those perpetrated by the State.

The book also draws on findings from a five-year project by the Central America Women's Network (CAWN)[2] working with the Centro de Estudios de la Mujer in Honduras (CEMH) to address violence against women and poverty in the most marginalized communities in Honduras, which ran for five years until 2011. Two co-authors of this book respectively wrote a ground-breaking report and a toolkit[3] on intersecting violences, with practical examples of how women's organizations, NGOs and community groups in Latin America were using an intersectional lens. They consider its innovations and positive results to be relevant today for the struggles of women's organizations in combatting and eradicating VAWG.

The conceptual framework and lessons from the CAWN/CEMH project are pertinent to this collection of case studies that examine successful activities in mitigating violence. The project in Honduras showed the effectiveness of taking a multi-layered approach to empowering women and enhancing their capacity to combat violence and improve their livelihoods. This approach included promoting gender equality through raising awareness among men and promoting non-violent masculinities; improving state services for women affected by violence; and influencing policy and decision makers in Honduras and internationally through research and advocacy. The project recognized women's initial situation as victims of violence when they joined in the activities but then, through awareness and mutual support, celebrated their role as survivors and agents of transformative change in their own contexts. Importantly, the project highlighted how women's experiences of violence need to be understood through an intersectional lens in order to develop appropriate responses. This enabled poor, semi-urban, and rural women to find a voice, stand up to violence, and participate in concrete solutions to the problems they faced. A key achievement was that women gained self-esteem and awareness of their rights, and many were able to represent their needs and ultimately take greater control over their lives and wellbeing.

Violence: a barrier to equal rights

Violence against women and girls (VAWG) is the extreme manifestation of sexism and gender discrimination which pervades all societies and countries cutting across social class, race, and ethnicity, among other expressions of discrimination. While poverty, conflict, and social crisis can trigger an increase in different forms of violence, they are not the only causes: unequal power relations, unfair distribution of wealth, unequal access to land, property, and productive resources also exacerbate VAWG in different contexts. State violence should also be considered when identifying different forms of violence against women and girls, especially in countries with authoritarian governments.

Violence affects women and girls in both private and public spaces: in their intimate relationships, in their working lives and economic activities, and in how they navigate their communities and the public sphere. At the household level, VAWG can have devastating consequences on families and communities, as it perpetuates a continuum of violence that affects all aspects of private and public life. VAWG can marginalize women from meaningful participation in political and community life and it also hampers women's power to influence policies that have a direct impact on their lives, livelihoods, and their fundamental human rights.

Because of the complexity of these factors, a wide range of policy responses and actions are required to protect women and girls from different forms of violence and abuse and to prevent VAWG from being perpetuated. In this book we present some of the inspiring and innovative strategies, campaigns, and activities women have undertaken to resist intersecting forms of violence in several Latin American countries and within the diaspora in the UK. We also look at successful actions by women's organizations to address VAWG at the policy level.

A transformative approach to VAWG

Women weaving powers from the ground

A successful approach in the CAWN/CEMH Honduras project was to move from a centralized and individualistic model of working on VAWG to a holistic, collective method with women taking centre stage as powerful agents of transformative change. These women became facilitators in processes of self-empowerment in their communities, standing up to the violence affecting their everyday lives. Another important component was sharing feminist narratives and proposals and increasing understanding among women in the participating organizations about the underlying causes that fuel violence and discrimination against them. This led to the research and publication of a groundbreaking report on intersecting violences (Muñoz Cabrera,

2010) and a toolkit (Thomson, 2011) with practical examples of how women's organizations, NGOs, and community groups in several Latin American countries were addressing issues of difference, exclusion, and discrimination. At the time, intersectionality was not well understood as a concept in the Latin American context, and there was a keen interest in applying this analysis to women's activism. The women's organizations involved found this research helped to strengthen their actions and activism in Honduras aimed at transforming their situation and protesting the social and institutional impunity surrounding VAWG.

The transformative approach of the project in Honduras was shown to be sustainable through the empowerment of disadvantaged women living in poverty, including poor Indigenous (Lenca) and Afro-Caribbean descendent (Garifuna[4]) women living in remote areas, as well as lesbian and trans women living in marginalized urban communities. Aspects of this transformative approach were the starting point for the subsequent King's College/LAB project with its focus on resistance, resilience, and new proposals that also need to be understood from an intersectional perspective.

An intersectional approach

Intersectional analysis exposes the many ways that women are marginalized because they are women - for example being members of a particular age group; geographical region; ethnic, religious, or linguistic minority; gender identity or sexual orientation - and it also uncovers the complexity of violence and discrimination against them. The original conceptualization of intersectionality came from the Combahee River Collective, a feminist socialist organization of Black lesbians in Boston (1975). It was further theorized by Kimberlé Williams Crenshaw (1991) and subsequently by other Black feminists in the US, such as Patricia Hill Collins (2009), in the context of understanding how racism - intersecting with gender and class discrimination - disempowered African American women in very distinctive ways.[5] The concept of intersectionality has also been developed by Latin American feminists such as Sueli Carneiro (2003), Beatriz Nascimento (2021) and others, especially those working within a decolonial feminist framework, such as María Lugones (2010) and Ochy Curiel (2013).

An intersectional lens identifies how issues of multiple forms of discrimination operate in complex ways and in different contexts, impinging on women's fundamental human rights, limiting their choices, and preventing equal access to resources and opportunities for participation in social, economic, and political life. Women from Indigenous groups are particularly vulnerable to intersecting violences because of their gender, socio-economic class, and ethnicity and they endure widespread stereotyping which is a legacy of colonial power. Even Indigenous and Black women who have roles in local authority systems or have been elected to positions of power are faced with violence and prejudice. Women living with some form of disability might have different needs and are possibly more vulnerable to violence than other women. The type of disability and their reliance on others for support can also affect their access to services and to justice for crimes committed against them. It is important to understand how discriminatory mechanisms intersect to further disempower women and girls who do not conform to normative standards of womanhood in post-colonial patriarchal and capitalist societies structured along lines of race, class, and gender. This analysis should therefore be integrated into appropriate responses to tackle different forms of violence.

Social and gender norms, as well as economic and political inequalities and the legacies of colonialism bolstered by the State are key drivers of VAWG in Latin America. Women's organizations are therefore calling for narratives, policies, and legislation that will contribute to reducing or at least mitigating different forms of VAWG and protect women's rights and bodily integrity.

Engaging with power

As the case studies in this book show, a root cause of VAWG is the unequal power relations between women and men.[6] This inequality is fuelled and perpetuated by patriarchy, racism, consumerist capitalism, and colonialism – systems which consolidate men's political, economic, social, and cultural dominance over women. They are also at the heart of dominant (and toxic) forms of masculinity, which accentuate inequality in access to and control over resources and decision-making in the household, in the market, and within public institutions.

In some Latin American countries, men have come together in a regional network called MenEngage América Latina[7] dominant ideals of masculinity and reject stereotypical masculine behaviours which condone violence. Some organizations, such as Instituto Promundo Brasil,[8] recognise the importance of working with boys from an early age to challenge and change unequal relations and violent behaviour. They also work with young people of all genders to find new patterns of equitable relationships for future generations. However, this is not enough. The shift of mindset and transformation of structural inequalities required to end VAWG must also take place at higher levels of decision making. Currently, policymakers, who are often representative of social and economic elites, design and implement policies which are detached from women's daily realities and hinder their enjoyment of fundamental rights on equal terms with men.

Economic policies stemming from the neoliberal model of economic development have also contributed to the web of VAWG and accentuated women's structural marginalization. This model has unleashed a new process of dispossession for poor, Indigenous, and Black women as they continue to be denied their right to land, property, decent work, and social services. These processes have been exacerbated by deep-seated colonial legacies that subjugate women, especially those of colour, and which also permeate the functioning of political, socioeconomic, and cultural systems throughout Latin America. The case studies presented in this book show that an intersectional approach increases understanding of the struggles of women against different forms of violence that are deeply embedded in patriarchal, neoliberal, colonial, and racist systems of power and oppression including economic violence and exploitation in the workplace.

The nature and extent of VAWG

The prevalence of multiple and intersecting forms of VAWG continues unabated and has become even more visible in the past decade. There is an alarming rise in femicides throughout Latin America, an increasing level of control of reproductive rights by state agencies, an upsurge of hate crimes against LGBTQ+ people, growing hostility toward migrant women including trafficking for sexual exploitation, and increased incidence and/or visibility of sexual harassment and abuse in the workplace and public spaces.

The World Health Organization (WHO) estimate that in Latin America overall, 25 per cent of women (55–66 million) experience intimate partner violence in their lifetimes and 12 per cent (an estimated 25-30 million) of women are subjected to non-partner violence in their lifetime[9] (WHO, 2018). Table 1 provides official statistics on VAWG in the region; however, it is not a complete picture as the data does not include younger girls and women over reproductive age who are also survivors of different forms of violence. There is a scarcity of disaggregated data as these statistics depend on women's self-reporting. The WHO and UN Women have recognized this and they began a five-year global programme (2018-2022) to strengthen methodologies for measuring violence against women and improve data collection at the country and regional levels. They have identified several constraints to reporting such as cultural norms which in some communities mean that there is an acceptability of violence by intimate partners, and that

Table I.1: Proportion of adult women experiencing physical and/or sexual violence by intimate partner (lifetime and last 12 months) in selected Latin American countries

Country	Lifetime physical and/or sexual intimate partner violence	Physical and/or sexual intimate partner violence in last 12 months
Argentina (2015)	27%	3%
Bolivia (2016)	58.5%	27%
Brazil (2018)	17%	3%
Colombia (2015)	33%	18%
Ecuador (2014)	40%	11%
El Salvador (2017)	14%	6%
Mexico (2016)	25%	9.5%
Peru (2017)	31%	11%
Uruguay (2013)	17%	3%

Source: Compiled from UN Women Global Database on Violence Against Women (2022)

women often do not report intimate partner violence to the police as this could make their situation even more difficult.

During the COVID-19 pandemic, an increase in levels and intensity of domestic and intra-family violence was reported throughout Latin America. Women living in poor urban neighbourhoods experienced especially high levels of domestic violence. For example, in the state of Rio de Janeiro, despite underreporting, available data showed more than 250 women were victims of violence every day during lockdown, amounting to 73,000 women between March and December 2020 alone, and 61 per cent of these cases occurred inside homes (ISP, 2021). There are also major differences within specific Latin American countries. For example, in Brazil *over half* of the 3,089 girls under the age of 14 who were raped in 2019 were Black (Wright, 2021). However, in general there is a lack of information and disaggregated data on the growing levels of violence among women, especially affecting Indigenous and Afro-descendant, migrant, and internally displaced women, as well as women living with some form of disability, those enduring human trafficking, and LQBTQ+ people, among others. For this reason, empirical data gathered on the ground is essential to give a better understanding of the extent of violence affecting different groups of women.

The pandemic also provoked a worrying increase in cyber-harassment, online bullying, stalking, and hate speech among women and girls throughout the continent. Although data is limited, a study by Plan International (2020) found that 60 per cent of girls and young women between the ages of 15-25 who participated in a survey in selected Latin American countries had experienced some form of online harassment on social media platforms. Social media harassment starts at a young age, with most girls saying that their first experience happened between the ages of 14-16 (Smit & Fraser, 2022). As well as adolescent girls and young women, others most at risk of online violence are human rights defenders, women in politics, journalists, bloggers, women belonging to ethnic minorities, Indigenous women, lesbian, bisexual, and transgender women, and women with disabilities (UN Women, 2020). Research in seven Latin American countries found that women journalists experienced high levels of abuse on social media, which has led to over two-thirds (68 per cent) of women journalists self-censoring and withdrawing from debates and online discussions (Cueller & Chaher, 2020).

Femicide is not a new phenomenon in Latin America but there has been a dramatic increase in the past decade, and it has been exacerbated since 2020 with.[10] For example, according to a report by Amnesty International, the killings of 3,723 women were registered in Mexico in 2020, although only 940 were investigated as feminicides (Amnesty International, 2021). Femicide is prevalent throughout the continent and these murders are often carried out deliberately and with extreme cruelty, frequently by partners or relatives of the victim. However, in other cases, young women have been killed by men connected to criminal gangs and drug and human trafficking activities. The extent to which these crimes represent acts of hatred towards women can be seen in the descriptions provided by women's organizations on the magnitude of the cruelty and torture of victims of femicides, as has been noted in the case of Guatemala.[11] From an intersectional perspective, it is also important to note that LQBTQ+ people are often the most likely to be murdered. For example, the Brazilian collective Grupo Gay da Bahia (Bahia Gay Group), notes that one LGBTQ+ person dies every hour in Brazil (cited in De Souza and Rodrigues Selis, 2022: 6). Also, in Brazil, it has been shown that rates of lesbocide have increased dramatically over recent years with an increase of 237 per cent between 2016 and 2017 (Davidson, 2019).

New and worrying forms of violence are being identified, for example, a recent report on trends in Latin America highlights a number of issues affecting girls and young women, such as widespread sexual harassment in public spaces and transport; a growing trend of online ICT-facilitated violence; school-related gender-based violence - while child and early forced marriage and unions are not recognized as a significant issue in several countries where the practice is common. With the increase of migration flows as a result of poverty, urban violence, and environmental disasters, women and girls are

Box I.1: Femicides in selected countries (2021)

Country	Number	Rate per 100,000 women
Argentina:	210	0.92
Chile:	52	0.52
Colombia:	622	2.40
Ecuador:	195	2.21
Uruguay:	30	1.67

The average age of the victims was 34 years. In most cases the crimes were perpetrated by a partner or ex-partner, another male relative or someone known to the victim. In only three cases the assailant was unknown. The majority were killed by a firearm or knives but there were other methods used such as burning, asphyxiation, torture, and poisoning.

Source: Mapa Latinoamericano de Feminicidios (MLF) (Mundosur, 2021)

increasingly at risk of trafficking for sexual and labour exploitation (Smit & Fraser, 2022).

Although racial and cultural violence against Indigenous and Afro-Descendant women is not new, there is much greater awareness of it than in the past. While these different forms of VAWG are being identified through research and advocacy by women's organizations and feminist scholars, they are being overlooked by policymakers and so it is essential to give increasing support to the women's movement and initiatives developed by grassroots women in particular. This is especially important in Latin America where incidence levels are extremely high, but also where there is potential for change in light of the strength of the women's movement in the continent.

Intersecting forms of violence and the impact of the pandemic on women's rights

In the case studies laid out in this book, we highlight specific issues affecting women from diverse social and economic backgrounds and origins in considering the prevalence of VAWG. Economic violence affects women workers in insecure employment and the COVID-19 pandemic has made these forms of violence more apparent, as well as intensifying intimate partner violence and gender inequalities and discrimination already widespread in Latin America. Indigenous women are economically vulnerable, especially in urban areas, where they usually work in the informal sector, for example as street traders or as domestic workers, and lockdown has prevented many from continuing with these income-generating activities. Women living in poverty are especially vulnerable to infection of the virus because their living conditions make it difficult to follow public health advice to stay indoors and ensure social distancing. Chapter 1 shows how women living in poverty in urban areas are especially vulnerable. Many live in overcrowded households and communities where there is no running water, or a scarcity of water, so constant handwashing is not possible. The regional office of UN Women in Panama also highlights the vulnerability of women employed in domestic work throughout Latin America due to the crisis caused by COVID-19, which is reported in Chapter 2. The pandemic had a disproportionate impact on women's lives, but it has not silenced their claims for equal access to justice and a shift towards non-discriminatory policies in the COVID-19 scenario.

Women's organizations have united and found common platforms and demands through regional networks during the pandemic, such as the Latin American and Caribbean Committee for the Defence of Women's Rights (Comité de América Latina y el Caribe para la Defensa de los Derechos de las Mujeres - CLADEM) which took a clear stance against VAWG during the pandemic[12], and the Latin American Network against Gender Violence (Red Latinoamericana contra la Violencia de Género), which widely disseminated a manifesto against the increased levels of violence endured by women during the pandemic.[13]

The lack of reproductive and sexual health rights in the region has led to many protests and campaigns by feminists and women's organizations in recent years. On the one hand, thanks to pressure mounted on governments by feminist campaigns, there has been progress on abortion rights in several countries such as Argentina, Colombia, and Mexico. On the other hand, conservative movements and governments have successfully pushed back against progress, making reproductive rights a battleground for women's bodily autonomy throughout the continent. Chapter 3 presents the ways in which repressive abortion policies and a lack of access to birth control and sex education expose many women and girls to heightened forms of violence against their bodily integrity. Responses to the COVID-19 pandemic have only exacerbated the problem, further reducing access to services. In addition, increased numbers of teenage and even pre-teen pregnancies during the period of the pandemic and quarantine provides evidence of the high levels of sexual violence against girls within their own homes and communities.

VAWG is multidimensional and can take many forms. For example, state, institutional, and police violence have been shown to target

Black women disproportionately throughout Latin America. As shown in Chapter 5, migrant Latin American women are often affected by racism, discrimination, and different forms of violence when residing in countries of the global North. Further reflection on structural factors is important in order to understand the continuum of VAWG – a concept first introduced by British professor Liz Kelly (1988) to show how multiple forms of gender-based violence, from exploitation and discrimination to rape and murder, exist along a continuum, all interlinked and reinforcing one another, rather than existing in a hierarchy. Consequently, a variety of actions are needed if we are to challenge unequal social relations, transform attitudes and practices, and change social values and institutions.

In their efforts to tackle state violence as a remnant of colonial legacies, some Indigenous women have developed a conceptual framework to distinguish specific forms of violence that affect them because of their ethnicity, race, social class, and the legacy of colonialism. This framework also includes the correlation between their human rights as women and as constitutive members of Indigenous communities. They denounce spiritual, symbolic, terri-torial, and environmental violence that go against their cultural beliefs and interactions with mother earth (see Chapter 4). The areas occupied by Indigenous people and farmers in many Latin American countries have become sites of extreme violence by police and private security guards acting to protect the interests of big business rather than those of the community. Women are standing alongside men in their communities against mining and deforestation and economic models that are destroying their native territories and depriving them of access to/and control of land, territory, and property.

Speaking back to power: resistance strategies and conceptual frameworks

Faced with a lack of action by authorities and the criminalization and stigmatization of women for protesting and claiming their rights, many women's organizations throughout the continent and beyond have resisted. This resistance has taken many forms, including strategies and conceptual frameworks defined by their lived experience of gendered and intersectional violence. Overall, these resistance strategies reinforce women's power for self and collective empowerment and for trans-formative agency. Examples of resistance frameworks are as diverse as the women who undertake them on the ground. Importantly, some of these have been documented by like-minded feminist scholars and activists, and some have been nourished by feminist thought. In the context of resistance being inherently about intersectional power relations (hooks, 1990), many Latin American feminists have been extremely influential in shaping challenges to male violence against women throughout the continent. Rita Segato's arguments (2016) around gendered violence in Latin America as a war against women's bodies rooted in interrelations between the colonial state, neoliberal capitalism, and patriarchy, have prompted many public forms of resistance, such as the widespread Rapist in Your Path (*Un violador en tu camino*) performances created by Las Tesis in Chile. Verónica Gago (2020) builds on Segato to argue that gender violence is multidimensional and such recognition allows for a questioning of the structures of this violence, generating resistance (see also De Souza & Rodrigues Selis, 2022).

The resistance strategies and frameworks of women's organizations and movements in Latin America can be summarised as follows:

Setting up observatories and mapping cases of femicide

Women's organizations are carrying out research and monitoring the situation regarding femicides: collecting data to make the crimes visible, creating public awareness, and advocating for state action to prevent and punish violent crimes against women in private and public spaces. Resistance strategies include claiming the State's accountability and challenging policy and law-makers to take more responsibility in protecting women and girls and preventing VAWG.

Latin American feminist activists who have been mapping gender-based violence and specifically femicides include María Salguero in Mexico, Ivonne Ramírez in Ciudad Juárez, Mexico, where rates of femicide are especially high, and Helena Suárez Val in Uruguay, as well as the Colectivo de Geografía Crítica in Ecuador.[14]

Mobilizing to expose, prevent, and punish gendered intersectional VAWG

Exposure: the extent of exploitation and discrimination of women across private and public spaces has become better known thanks to the painstaking efforts of women's rights and feminist organizations to document, expose, and raise awareness of the everyday forms of violence they endure in their households, communities, and society at large. Their struggle has also exposed economic forms of VAWG that are often overlooked in official policy documents. This includes not being able to decide on the use of income that women themselves generate and bring to the household and, on a broader level, being dispossessed of their right to their bodies, territories, and livelihoods by the structural violence resulting from land grabbing.

Prevention and punishment: resistance actions and campaigns to transform the power structures of society and gender stereotypes include: working with young people and policy/decision-makers (including state actors) to change attitudes and behaviour; awareness-raising activities with men and women in their diversity; strengthening gender/intersectional responsive policy implementation and law enforcement; pushing for a rigorous policy of prevention of VAWG and punishment of perpetrators of VAWG aimed at reaching zero tolerance of violence.

Campaigning for protection against VAWG and provision of justice to survivors

Protection: actions to support women survivors of violence include education and information on rights (legal literacy); training the police, the judiciary, local authorities, and health service professionals; and legal advice and support for victims of violent crime going through legal processes. Actions to ensure the protection of victims of VAWG include advocacy activities for policy implementation and the enforcement of existing legislation.

Provision: resistance strategies include setting up refuges and income generation activities and organizing varied actions to demand governments and local and regional authorities provide women-friendly, properly resourced services that empower women and help them to survive and fight back, and address improved service provision and delivery.

Resilience and coping strategies

An important dimension of resilience is that in critical circumstances, women's power to resist stems from their lived experience of violence and is often forged collectively. Women at the grassroots have been actively weaving collective empirical knowledge and actions to overcome challenges, criminalization, stigmatization, life threats and hopelessness – often in situations of extreme danger. In cases where human rights defenders have been murdered, such as the cases of Berta Cáceres and Marielle Franco (see Chapters 4 and 1), other women have continued the pathways of emancipatory knowledge left behind by their peers.

Women have built collective proposals to counter the constraints, threats and challenges they face daily, for example through self-help groups; self-defence training, and counselling. WhatsApp groups serve to alert peers of possible dangers, help women avoid feeling alone with their troubles, and facilitate the arrangement of support for those unable to ensure food security for themselves and their families.

Coping strategies also include self and collective healing (mental and physical), and staying positive and motivating others to keep going and stay organized and focused when things go wrong. Reclaiming historically discarded knowledges/epistemologies is key for Indigenous, Afro-descendant and Quilombola women[15] struggling at the grassroots. Others cope by creating emotional-political communities against intimate, state, and institutional violence, through sharing personal testimonies and creating emotional bonds that may then be reconfigured into political action (Jimeno, 2010; McLeod & de Marini, 2018).

Importantly, the resistance paradigms developed by women at the grassroots has also drawn on and intersects with the support of like-minded allies (civil society organizations, feminist scholars, and activists) as in the creative memorialization actions presented in Chapter 6.

Women's organizations have always and continue to take a range of actions to denounce and mitigate the disempowering effects of different forms of gendered and intersectional violence, which we present in the case studies. The #NiUnaMenos protest which began in Argentina in 2015 and rapidly spread throughout Latin America, continues today as a vibrant social movement, showing that women are not afraid to stand up to violence and are demanding social change. Despite the restrictions of movement imposed by governments during the COVID-19 pandemic, thousands of women throughout the continent erupted into the streets over the past two years to protest against violence, and in several instances the demonstrators were violently stopped by the police and women arrested.

Ensuring equal access to justice: policy implementation and law enforcement

Throughout Latin America, governments have ratified international human rights conventions such as CEDAW, and national legal instruments are in force to prevent and punish VAWG, much of which is underpinned by feminist research, mobilizing and campaigning. However, these violations continue and indeed have generally increased in worrying new dimensions during the pandemic.

In 1995, the Inter-American Convention on the Prevention, Punishment, and Eradication of Violence against Women - better known as the Belém do Pará Convention - came into force and has since been ratified by 32 countries in the region. It is a legally binding international treaty that criminalizes all forms of violence and hate actions against women, especially sexual violence. In 2004 a mechanism was established by the OAS to ensure the State parties' compliance with the Convention. However, despite many legal frameworks, implementation remains low and impunity for perpetrators is common throughout the region. Compounding this issue, only scarce public funding is allocated to the structural improvement of courts and to gender-responsive capacity-building for justice officers across the continent.

Courts of Conscience have been used in recent decades in Latin America to denounce sexual violence as a weapon of war and highlight the impact of sexual aggressions and other multiple violations on women, especially in Central America and in Colombia. Ethical tribunals to denounce violations of women's human rights by transnational companies have also been organized in Chile by the National Association of Rural and Indigenous women (Asociación Nacional de Mujeres Rurales e Indígenas – ANAMURI). Although these courts are mainly ethical and do not have any judicial power, they have created spaces for women workers' individual and collective empowerment, and had important repercussions at a political level by making violence against women more visible. They have also given a voice to predominantly Indigenous and rural women at the grassroots to publicly denounce violent acts against them.[16]

Legal recognition is without doubt an important advancement in the judicial and political spheres, giving a framework for advocacy and for women's groups to put forward their demands for a life free from violence. However, it is questionable whether gender justice can be guaranteed without a radical reform of the power systems that reproduce patriarchal and intersectional violence. There are some grounds for optimism, as recent research (for example from Htun & Jensenius in Mexico, 2022) has shown that anti-VAWG legislation can bring about some positive social change, even if limited. Similarly in Nicaragua, research over three decades suggests that policy reforms resulting from feminist advocacy led to a decrease in VAWG (Ellsberg, Quintanilla & Ugarte, 2022). Although in recent years this progress was curtailed by the authoritarian Ortega regime which has attacked the women's movement, imprisoned women leaders, and closed many NGOs working on women's rights.

Where is transformative change happening?

By transformative change we mean a shift to policies and practices that recognize intersectional diversity, that are enshrined in the principle of non-discrimination, and that guarantee the full exercise of the fundamental human rights of all women, in their rich diversity, and on equal terms with men. Throughout Latin America, women of different ages, sexualities, ethnic, racial, social, and cultural backgrounds are mobilizing and communicating like never before.

The struggle is not only around enforcement of laws and new policies, but also in changing power relations and addressing structural and state violence. Women's organizations are moving from individual empowerment to weaving a chain of voices that is spreading emancipatory knowledge and empowering pathways for women's political, economic, and social agency. This is occurring despite the devastating impact the COVID-19 pandemic has had on them, as illustrated in the case studies in this book. For example, the Quintana Roo Feminist Network in Mexico staged a sit-in at the State Congress for 94 days at the start of 2021, which led to legislators agreeing to hold a vote on the legalization of abortion. Although that vote was lost, it helped the movement to take the fight to the Supreme Court, and eventually the government approved a law on abortion which will have major ramifications for sexual and reproductive rights in Mexico.[17] The Latin American Confederation of Household Workers is also running a regional campaign to end harassment in the workplace, as part of a global campaign (see Chapter 2). In the UK, Latin American women formed a network of migrant women's organizations called Step up Migrant Women to influence policymakers and make changes in a new domestic violence bill to take account of the vulnerability of migrant women survivors of violence (see Chapter 5).

Despite all the progress made by feminists, women's organizations and movements to tackle VAWG at different levels, it is an ongoing struggle to address different forms of violence and to support survivors and their families.

Grassroots women's organizations have difficulties funding their activities and many operate on a voluntary basis. The international funding model in place for over a decade has had an adverse impact on the women's movements in Latin America because larger INGOs were prioritized by donors, with small local women's organizations being subcontracted to deliver NGO projects. A technical, results-based approach was introduced, which made it harder to fund awareness-raising and advocacy activities. To obtain funding, women's organizations had to become NGOs themselves to comply with donor priorities. Small women's organizations often do not have the infrastructure or expertise to meet donors' technical demands, making it difficult to apply for grants, and so they have made strategic alliances with international NGOs to carry out joint projects. Additionally, Latin America as a whole is considered 'middle income' and its constituent countries are no longer considered the poorest – and therefore priority – countries for international aid, leading to a lack of financial support for women's organizations in the region. This ignores the vast income and social inequalities within countries in the region. Because of this criteria, many international NGOs who had been operating in Latin America were forced to pull out or to reduce their programmes due to these funding priorities, making it more difficult for small women's organizations to be supported in their work to end violence against women and girls.

Nonetheless, women's grassroots networks are organizing and making changes, and in the chapters that follow, we present some of the activities, strategies, and campaigns women are using to fight back against intersecting forms of violence. We examine the impact of gendered and intersectional forms of violence in different countries and communities in Latin America and women's resistance to them, in a range of different settings. We also showcase different approaches, innovative projects, and actions on VAWG taken by women's organizations, which transform women's lives and push for structural change. Importantly, the chapters bring to the fore the testimonies and the voices of women leaders who are taking forward the fight to challenge gendered and intersectional violence and who are making their voices heard in different spheres of influence.

Notes

1. We refer to the podcast Women Resisting Violence throughout the book. It was published in 2022 by Latin America Bureau, produced by Louise Morris in collaboration between LAB and King's College London and funded by the ESRC Impact Acceleration Account held at King's College London, with additional support from the National Lottery Community Fund. Listen at wrv.org.uk/podcast
2. CAWN was a UK solidarity network and NGO based in London which supported women's organizations in Central America from 1992–2017. It was forced to close due to lack of funding and resources for their work.
3. See Muñoz Cabrera (2010) and Thomson (2011).
4. Garifuna are descendants of an Afro-Indigenous population from the Caribbean who were exiled to the Honduran coast in the eighteenth century and who also live in Belize.
5. See UN Women (2020) 'Intersectional feminism: what it means and why it matters', available from: https://www.unwomen.org/en/news/stories/2020/6/explainer-intersectional-feminism-what-it-means-and-why-it-matters

6. We use the terms women and men while recognising that there are more than two genders and that trans and non-binary people are also subjected to discrimination and violence. But our main focus in this book is highlighting the violence that affects cis-gender women (women who identify with the gender they were assigned according to their sex at birth).

7 MenEngage Latin America is an alliance of organizations dedicated to working on transforming patriarchal masculinities and engaging men and boys in gender equality. It currently has 110 members in 12 Latin American countries. See more at: https://www.redmasculinidadeslac.org/inicio/

8. Founded in 1997, Promundo Brasil is an NGO operating in different regions of Brazil and other countries globally, seeking to promote gender equality and the prevention of violence with a focus on the involvement of men and women in the transformation of masculinities. More on their violence prevention work at: https://promundo.org.br/trabalho/?programa=prevencao-de-violencia

9. Statistics are available on the UN Women global database (2016) https://evaw-global-database.unwomen.org/en

10. The first cases of what became known in Mexico and Central America as femicide (*femicidio/ feminicidio* in Spanish) or the killing of women because they are women, emerged in 1993 in Ciudad Juárez in Mexico. Reports began to appear in the press of increasing numbers of women's mutilated bodies being discovered and of many women disappearing in the city, many of these were young women workers in the manufacturing factories in the free trade zones.

11. See Wallace (2021).

12. See for more information 'Violencia de género la otra pandemia' (CLADEM, 2020) https://cladem.org/wp-content/uploads/2020/11/Violencia-de-Genero-la-otra-pandemia-25N2020.pdf

13. Full manifesto ('Manifiesto Latinoamericano contra las violencias de género, femicidios/ feminicidios y los trans/travesticidios') available at https://mundosur.org/wp-content/uploads/2020/06/Manifiesto-Latinoamericano.pdf

14. See María Salguero's mapping of femicide in Mexico at https://feminicidiosmx.crowdmap.com/; maps of Ciudad Juárez via Ellas Tienen Nombre at http://www.ellastienennombre.org; maps of femicide in Uruguay at http://feminicidiouruguay.net; and Ecuador's Colectivo de Geografía Crítica at https://www.google.com/maps/d/u/0/viewer?mid=1GJGbiCYkTZUS2ryoq3tCiW4txBs&ll=-1.421683061887858%2C-78.91224145000001&z=6

15. Quilombola women are Afro-Brazilian women who reside in settlements (quilombolos) historically established by escaped enslaved people, their ancestors, through organized territorial resistance.

16. See for more: Sierra, Maria Teresa & Figueroa Romero, Dolores, (2020) Indigenous Women Break the Silence and Demand Justice Court of Conscience on Gender Violence in Mexico. ABYA-YALA: revista sobre acesso à justiça e direitos nas américas. https://www.academia.edu/49460881/Mujeres_ind%C3%ADgenas_rompen_el_silencio_Tribunales_de_Conciencia_en_Guerrero
17. See Lines (2021), 'Quintana Roo sit-in marks historic step towards legalisation of abortion in Mexico', https://lab.org.uk/quintana-roo-sit-in-marks-historic-step-towards-legalisation-of-abortion-in-mexico

Bibliography

Amnesty International (2021) 'Justice on trial: failures in criminal investigations of feminicides preceded by disappearance in the State of Mexico', *AMR* 41/4556/2021, https://www.amnesty.org/en/documents/amr41/4556/2021/en

Carneiro, S. (2003) 'Mulheres em movimento', *Estudos Avançados* 17(49), pp. 117–32

Carneiro, S. et al. (2017) 'Ennegrecer el feminismo', in Campoalegre Septien, R. and Bidaseca, K. (eds.) *Más allá del decenio de los pueblos afrodescendientes.* CLACSO, pp. 109–16, https://doi.org/10.2307/j.ctv253f4nn.10

CLADEM (2020) 'Violencia de género la otra pandemia' *Pronunciamiento,* 25 November, https://cladem.org/wp-content/uploads/2020/11/Violencia-de-Genero-la-otra-pandemia-25N2020.pdf

Collins, P.H. (2009) *Black feminist thought: knowledge, consciousness, and the politics of empowerment.* London: Routledge.

Combahee River Collective (1977) 'The Combahee River Collective statement', https://www.reed.edu/cres/assets/Combahee-River-Collective,-Black-Feminist-Statement,-How-We-Get-Free---Taylor.pdf

Crenshaw, K. (1991) 'Mapping the margins: intersectionality, identity politics, and violence against women of color', *Stanford Law Review* 43, pp. 1241–99. See also her video on intersectionality at https://youtu.be/hBaIhlmM3ow

Cuellar L. and Chaher, S. (2020) 'Being a journalist on Twitter: digital gender violence in Latin America', https://www.dropbox.com/s/8aq93cki5raokxp/Ser%20periodista%20en%20Twitter_Cuellar-Chaher-%28SUMMARY-%20INGL%C3%89S%29.pdf?dl=0

Davidson, M. (2019) 'Necropolítica lesbocida: uma análise sobre o necrobiopoder, soberania e violências contra lésbicas no contexto Bolsonarista', *Revista Itaca* 34, https://revistas.ufrj.br/index.php/Itaca/article/view/30469

de Souza, N.M.F. and Rodrigues Selis, L.M. (2022) 'Gender violence and feminist resistance in Latin America', *International Feminist Journal of Politics* 24:1, pp. 5–15, https://doi.org/10.1080/14616742.2021.2019483.

Ellsberg, M., Quintanilla, M. and Ugarte, W.J. (2022) 'Pathways to change: three decades of feminist research and activism to end violence against women in Nicaragua', *Global Public Health*, https://doi.org/10.1080/17441692.2022.2038652

Gago, V. (2020) *Feminist International.* London: Verso.

Gouveia, R. and Groisman, D. (2020) 'Helena Hirata: "A questão da interseccionalidade ampliou muito o escopo das análises já feitas anteriormente"', CADTM, 2 March, https://www.cadtm.org/Helena-Hirata-A-questao-da-interseccionalidade-ampliou-muito-o-escopo-das

Hooks, b. (1990) 'Marginality as a site of resistance', in: Ferguson, R., Gever, M., Minh-ha, T. and West, C. (eds.) *Out there: marginalization and contemporary cultures.* New York: MIT Press, pp. 341–343

Htun, M. and Jensenius, F. (2022) 'Expressive power of anti-violence legislation: changes in social norms on violence against women in Mexico', *World Politics* 74(1), pp. 1–36

ISP – Instituto de Segurança Pública (2021) 'Monitor da violência doméstica e familiar contra a mulher no período de isolamento social', http://www.ispvisualizacao.rj.gov.br/monitor/index.html

Jimeno, M. (2010) 'Emoções e política: A vítima e a construção de comunidades emocionais', *Mana* 16(1), pp. 99–121

Kelly, L. (1998) *Surviving sexual violence.* Oxford: Polity

Lugones, M. (2010) 'Toward a decolonial feminism', *Hypatia* 25(4), pp. 742–759

Macleod, M. and De Marinis, N. (eds.) (2018) *Resisting violence: emotional communities in Latin America.* Basingstoke: Palgrave Macmillan

Merino, C. (2011), interviewed by Patricia Muñoz Cabrera, 8 April, Ecuador

Mundosur (2021), Mapa Latinoamericano de feminicidios (MLF), https://mundosur.org/feminicidios

Mundosur (2020) 'Manifiesto Latinoamericano contra las violencias de género, femicidios/ feminicidios y los trans/travesticidios', https://mundosur.org/wp-content/uploads/2020/06/Manifiesto-Latinoamericano.pdf

Muñoz Cabrera, P. (2010) *Intersecting violences: a review of feminist debates and theoretical approaches on violence against women and poverty in Latin America.* London: CAWN

Nascimento, B. (2021) 'The concept of quilombo and black cultural resistance', in: Smith, C., Davies, A. and Gomes, B., '"In front of the world": translating Beatriz Nascimento', *Antipode* 53(1), pp. 279–316

Romero, D. (2018) 'Morna Macleod y Natalia de Marinis (2018) 'Resisting violence. Emotional communities in Latin America' (Resistiendo a la violencia: comunidades emocionales en América Latina)', *Cultura y Representaciones Sociales* 13(25), https://www.culturayrs.unam.mx/index.php/CRS/article/view/623/pdf

Segato, R.L. (2016) 'Patriarchy from "margin to center"', *South Atlantic Quarterly* 115(3), pp.615–624

Sierra, M. and Figueroa Romero, M. (2021) 'Mujeres indígenas rompen el silencio y exigen justicia tribunal de conciencia sobre violencia de género en México', http://dx.doi.org/10.26512/abyayala.v4i1.32380

Smit, H. and Fraser, E. (2022) 'Latin America regional analysis', *What Works to Prevent Violence,* https://ww2preventvawg.org/sites/default/files/2022-07/Ending%20VAWC%20HD%20Report%2010%20Latin%20America%20GBV%20trends%20May%202022%20FINAL.pdf

Thomson, M. (2011) *Putting intersectional analysis into practice toolkit.* London: CAWN

UN Women (2016) 'Global database on violence against women', https://evaw-global-database.unwomen.org/en/countries

UN Women (2020) 'Intersectional feminism: what it means and why it matters', 1 July, https://www.unwomen.org/en/news/stories/2020/6/explainer-intersectional-feminism-what-it-means-and-why-it-matters

Wallace, S. (2021) 'Guatemala: lasting legacy of gender-based violence and state impunity. *Latin America Bureau,* 25 November, https://lab.org.uk/wrv-guatemala-legacy-gender-based-violence

WHO (2018) 'Violence against women prevalence estimates, 2018 – global fact sheet', https://www.who.int/publications/i/item/WHO-SRH-21.6

Wright, A. (2021) 'Understanding violence against women and girls in Brazil', *Latin America Bureau,* 24 September, https://lab.org.uk/understanding-violence-against-women-and-girls-in-brazil

CHAPTER 1

'They wanted to bury us, but they didn't know we were seeds': Resisting intersectional gendered violence against women in cities

Cathy McIlwaine and Moniza Rizzini Ansari

The title of this chapter relates to a Mexican proverb that was widely adopted in Brazil after the murder of Marielle Franco to show that women would not be silenced, but instead, would fight back. It also highlights the importance of acknowledging that urban violence in Latin America is deeply gendered and intersectional. Indeed, it is often characterized by the actions of armed gangs, state security forces, militias, and other forms of male-dominated organized groups. Much less attention is paid to how gendered intersectional violence against women and girls is implicated within urban violence.[1]

This chapter explores how women in the urban margins of cities interact with and are affected by armed urban violence on a daily basis. However, rather than focusing on women's vulnerability to gendered urban violence, we highlight women's agency in building their own practices of resistance through individual short-term coping mechanisms, as well as longer-term collective initiatives that place a feminist ethics of care at their centre. While we include examples from across Latin America, our specific focus is the work of the community-based organization Casa das Mulheres da Maré, the Maré Women's House in Rio de Janeiro, Brazil[2] (which is part of Redes da Maré organization) and which ties in closely with our podcast series. Casa das Mulheres runs a range of projects to challenge gender-based violence including more 'traditional' culinary and sewing programmes to improve women's livelihoods, legal and emotional support for survivors of violence through a clinic, and other forms of prevention work. Particularly during the ongoing COVID-19 pandemic, the ways that women in Maré organized to deal with rising levels of domestic violence and household hardship provide important insights into forms of resisting intersectional violence against women in cities.

What does intersectional gendered urban violence mean for women?

Gangs and armed militias, drug trafficking, gun crimes, clashes with police and other security forces – these masculinized depictions of urban violence as a major phenomenon in Latin American cities in recent decades rarely mention or portray women. This is partly because so much gendered violence occurs or is assumed to occur behind closed doors in the home, often making it invisible and tolerated. Although there have been important international policy commitments addressing violence against women in general, such as the Belem do Pará Convention (1995) (see Introduction), those focusing on urban violence against women have fallen short. For example, UN Women's (2017) Safe Cities and Safe Public Spaces initiative generally focuses on sexual harassment in public spaces, with limited consideration of its connection to wider forms of urban violence or the need to link the private and public spheres.

In order to understand urban violence, we must acknowledge its gendered and intersectional nature, recognizing women and girls as survivors and/or bystanders who also deal with its ramifications in their daily lives. Although young men, and especially poor Black men from marginalized backgrounds, are frequently the main victims of lethal urban violence, it is worth stressing that 36 per cent of women have experienced non-partner sexual violence or intimate partner violence (physical and/or sexual) globally (WHO, 2018), and that it has been suggested that women are twice as likely to experience violence in cities, especially in the global South (McIlwaine, 2013).

This is particularly insidious in the case of women living on the urban margins such as in 'slum' communities in Latin American cities – *favelas* in Brazil, *campamentos* in Chile, *pueblos jóvenes* in Peru, *colonias populares* in Mexico, *cantegriles* in Uruguay, *barrios populares* in Colombia, among many others. Here, women are affected in distinctive ways by urban violence, and this is marked by the social complexity and diverse demographics of these areas in terms of gender, race, class, and armed conflict. It is women who are exposed to hostile actions on the part of state agents knowing that the male members of their family are more likely to be wronged; it is women who assume strategic roles of defending their community and speaking up against police incursions; it is women who typically protect other families' children during cross-fire situations; and it is women who need to negotiate their mobility and safety in public and private spaces in order to move freely in urban areas. To keep safe in cities, women often develop strategies and practices of silence, body awareness, and online communication (see later in this chapter).

While women from all backgrounds suffer gender-based violence, those enduring intersectional gendered oppression and discrimination are more likely to experience this violence in more extreme ways. Statistics repeatedly show that due to colonial legacy, Indigenous and Afro-descendant women, including Quilombolas, are disproportionately affected by gendered violence. A large body of work has revealed how racism (reflected in anti-Black state violence and specifically police violence) in poor urban communities has severe long-term consequences for Black women – affective and deadly (Carneiro, 2003). This is especially severe in Brazil, where it has been termed 'anti-Black genocide' (Smith, 2017). In addition, it is often the case that Afro-descendant and/or LQBTQ+ women disproportionately experience gendered violence (Krenzinger et al., 2018; Krenzinger et al. 2021). Estimates even suggest that one LGBTQ+ person dies every 19 hours in Brazil, often in urban areas, ranking Brazil the worst country in the world for this kind of violence (de Souza & Rodrigues Selis, 2022: 6).

These forms of violence often shockingly play out in cities like Rio de Janeiro. Reports suggest that in Rio 17 women a day are victims of femicide and sexual violence.[3] In recent research in Maré, a Rio neighbourhood formed by the merging of 16 favelas, more than three-quarters of women said that violence against them occurred on a regular basis, while 57 per cent stated they had experienced it personally. Young Black women were most likely to experience it (69 per cent of Black women compared to 55 per cent of mixed-race and 50 per cent of those identifying as white). Lethal violence also plays out in insidious ways, forcing increasingly more women to become the sole heads of households in urban margins of cities (McIlwaine, 2021a).[4]

Besides direct harm, gendered violence can affect women in urban areas in invisible ways. The anxiety and fear women feel while navigating urban spaces itself constrains their right to the city, even before any case of direct violence takes place. Fear is also embodied in what feminist authors like Keisha-Khan Perry (2013) have called 'slow violence' or a 'slow death' of pain, anxiety and depression, particularly felt by mothers in Brazil whose children have been killed or injured. Others such as Christen Smith have used the term 'lingering trauma', to refer to the long-lasting physical and emotional effects of widespread, often state-sanctioned violence – particularly felt by Black women.[5] Women are also immediately affected as partners, wives, and mothers who will have to take sole responsibility for their families' livelihoods. Other layers of intersectional discrimination – including sexual orientation and gender identity, body-image standards (Afro hair, dark skin, language and accent, way of dressing), religious practice

Figure 1.1: Observational drawing of the everyday intersectional oppressions experienced by women in Maré, Rio de Janeiro, based on a focus group with five women. Credit: Mila de Choch. (McIlwaine, 2022a)

(Afro-Latin American faiths and rituals being mainly stigmatized) and markers of political activity – make people more likely to be further exposed to these forms of long-lasting violence. Underpinning these forms of intersectional and gendered violence is violence perpetrated by the State and especially the police. Figure 1 highlights some of the everyday intersectional oppression that women in Maré experience, and highlights how trans women, lesbians, those who are more masculine, and poor women are more exposed to such violence.

Another effect of the trauma and fear that women experience in cities is reflected in their reluctance to disclose and report cases of gender-based violence. Research in Maré reveals that just over half (52 per cent) of women who had experienced gender-based abuse disclosed or reported it. And when they did, it was almost always to informal sources of support (83 per cent), with only 2.5 per cent reporting to a formal source like the police (Krenzinger et al., 2018; McIlwaine et al., 2020). Women's reluctance to report can be explained by the lack of trust they have in public institutions, and the distress they feel when anticipating being re-victimized because of stigma against survivors of violence – particularly when geographical, racial, and class-related prejudices intersect to further disempower them. Compounded by women's lack of knowledge about their rights, other forms of passive and active exclusion from support can also be understood as gendered violence. Research in a range of contexts has shown how state services for women survivors of gendered violence often fail them, introducing new dimensions of victim-blaming and shaming. This is exacerbated by inadequate access to safe urban infrastructures like street lighting and public transport - which itself can be described as a form of 'infrastructural violence' but also leads to further perpetration of direct violence against women. This constellation of barriers means that women are often forced to turn to armed actors as alternative enforcers of justice, particularly against perpetrators of domestic violence (McIlwaine et al., 2021).

From an intersectional perspective, therefore, broader social problems such as poverty, inequality, and exclusion underpin gendered urban violence. In other words, forms of structural and symbolic violence rooted in racism, sexism, and discrimination reinforce direct and indirect violence against women. Indeed, the horrific realities of 'femicide' (killing women because of their gender) and 'feminicide' (where the State is implicated directly and indirectly in the killings) in Latin America have been integral in highlighting the relations between patriarchal and misogynistic norms and wider structural and institutional violence and racism. However, it is also important to point out that Latin American academics and activists have been key to lobbying for femicide to be defined as a crime, and they have achieved classification of femicide in 18 countries - even if this excludes the many forms of direct and indirect violence women endure. A key figure who was a victim of feminicide, but who also epitomizes challenges to the intersectional nature of gendered urban violence, was the late Marielle Franco (see Box 1.1).

Box 1.1: Marielle Franco: legacy of challenging intersectional, gendered, and urban violence

Marielle Franco was a remarkable activist from Maré in Rio de Janeiro who was killed in 2018 in a case that shocked the world. She embodied all the markers that lead thousands of women to be directly affected by urban violence in Brazil: a Black woman from a poor background; a *favelada*, born and raised in Maré; the mother of a 19-year-old daughter; a human rights activist from a socialist party (PSOL) elected as a politician; and the wife of Monica Benicio, who also became an elected councilwoman.

As a councillor, Marielle was a spokesperson for minorities. She advocated 'for the LGBTQ+ community, for the dignity of favela dwellers, for women in general, for the human rights of all Rio's citizens, including the right of young Black men to not be shot dead as suspects by violent, gun-happy policemen'. One of her main agendas before her death was to end police brutality and the widespread extrajudicial killings that occur in Rio's favelas. Days before her own assassination, she had accused the military police of killing two young men and terrorizing residents in the Acari favela.

Marielle was killed on 14 March 2018, aged 38, in a targeted political assassination allegedly by former policemen and members of a militia group in Rio de Janeiro. Although formed as paralegal or parastate groups, the militia are far from external to the state structures. Instead, the state apparatus is an active part of urban violence in Rio de Janeiro, with many Afro-Brazilian feminists adopting the term 'genocidal State' to refer to the '*genocídio do povo negro*' (the genocide of the Black population). Marielle's death reverberated through the world, but her case is still to be solved by the formal justice system. We do not know exactly who ordered her assassination and no one has yet been accused of or prosecuted for the crime.

The four bullets that killed Marielle have been seen to stand 'one each for racism, misogyny, homophobia and impunity'. However, her legacy is incredibly strong, not least as she represented many minorities and was a pioneer for women in marginalized communities. To evoke the Mexican proverb adopted in the protests in Brazil following Marielle's death and increasingly more disseminated in other Latin American countries: '*tentaram nos enterrar nos matar, mas não sabiam que éramos sementes*' (they wanted to bury us, but they didn't know we were seeds). Like flowers blooming from unknown dormant seeds, in the aftermath of Marielle's death, dozens of Black women from urban peripheries were elected council members in Brazilian cities as well as in the national congress. They are often referred to as Marielle's seeds, having co-signed a commitment to defend anti-racist, feminist, and popular agendas designated the 'Marielle Franco Agenda'.

Sources: Garayo Willemyns (2021); House (2015); Loureiro (2021); Rocha (2018)

Resisting gendered urban violence through coping practices and strategies

Although it is important to draw attention to the insidious and intersectional ways women suffer urban violence in Latin America, it is also crucial to acknowledge that women have agency through building ingenious practices and strategies of resistance to violence of many kinds. (Note that practices tend to be more reactive while strategies are more pre-determined.) While resistance can mean many things in this context, broadly speaking it entails acts, moments, or interventions to address or reduce violence. This might be in the form of short-term and reactive coping mechanisms or longer-term initiatives (formal or informal) which lead to wider structural and transformative change. Such resistance practices and strategies are also inherently intersectional and reflect wider power relations.

In Maré in Rio de Janeiro, women have been the driving force behind the neighbourhood's urban formation from the outset. In the 1980s, Maré was formed from community struggles for basic urban infrastructures and against urban inequality, much of which was led by remarkable women. According to Eliana Sousa Silva, speaking in the Women Resisting Violence podcast (2022): 'When I talk about the struggles we have faced in Maré, I am talking about a place where, behind any victory we have here, from the 80s', from the moment, for example, that I became President of the residents' association, there has not been a single fight that does not have women behind it, making it happen.' Eliana was the first woman to lead a neighbourhood association in her twenties, and later founded Redes da Maré in 1997.

Women in Maré have since continued to share important achievements collectively, challenging historical social injustices and developing key community knowledge. Specifically in relation to gendered urban violence, women in Maré use similar coping practices that routinely defy violence at a micropolitical level. They take action in order to protect themselves and others, whether this be through 'small acts' (Pain, 2014) or active resistance for dealing with both intimate partner and police and armed gang violence (McIlwaine et al., 2022a).

These practices effectively respond to fear, dangers, or actual violence through knowledge of local codes and can be hidden from outsiders' perspectives. For example, women make very conscious decisions about how to occupy spaces and locate themselves strategically. In public transport or public spaces, especially at night, they often choose to sit near other women and form a silent and momentary network of strangers. They might also carry sharp objects with them, as well as share their location with others through digital media devices. These survival tactics produce immediate results that might not produce longer term safety for women, but they allow women to avoid risks through calculating their navigation routes and sharing or checking real-time information about places or events in social media channels, such as Facebook and WhatsApp groups and safety apps (see also Box 1.2).

Box 1.2: Safetipin in Bogotá

Safetipin is a social organization founded in India in 2013 by Kalpana Viswanath, but now operating in 65 cities across the world with the aim of making public spaces safer for women. It does this through collecting large-scale data on safety using mobile phone apps, in order to raise awareness and reduce street harassment. The Safetipin app uses crowd-sourced data to identify safe and unsafe areas of the city. App users rate the space according to a set of parameters including lighting, openness, visibility, crowdedness, security, footpaths, availability of public transport, gender diversity, and feeling. For each, there's a grading system: green for safer areas, orange for less safe areas, and red for unsafe areas. Safetipin have developed three variations of the mobile phone app: My Safetipin; Safetipin Nite, and Safetipin Site. As well as benefiting users, who can make informed decisions about their movement in the city, Safetipin works with key public and private sector stakeholders to influence urban planning and assist in locating where additional lighting, police presence, or accessibility routes are required.

Bogotá was the first city in Latin America to use the Safetipin app in 2014, through a collaboration with the District Secretary for Women supported by UN Habitat and Cities Alliance. Using My Safetipin and Safetipin Nite, by 2019, 40,492 audit pins had been collected for roads covering 16,145 kms together with 3,843 audit pins for cycle routes covering 537 kms. Information gathered from the first phase of Safetipin was used to prioritize local and municipal infrastructure investment in street lighting, CCTV cameras, and the rebuilding of pathways to ensure better access. Safetipin data has also been used to mainstream gender into Bogotá public policy in relation to land use planning and security plans.

In 2016, the Women's District Secretariat conducted multiple sessions themed as 'Women taking the night' at sites close to public spaces identified as unsafe for women at nighttime. The aim was to make the night symbolically safe for women using performance, music, and art to raise awareness of women's right to live free from violence. 1,978 men and women participated in the campaign.

Safetipin therefore allows women to cope with violence in the public space in the short-term but their data also informs wider changes in mainstreaming women's safety in urban planning and private and public institutions.

Source: Viswanath and Basu (2015)

Linked with this, women will also often reveal a strategic use of their body language and voices in ways that might seem contradictory at first sight. For example, speaking loudly to draw attention from people around them or adopting silence to stay out of the spotlight from potential threats. Other embodied tactics emerge, spanning from habits of self-care (including physical exercise and beauty routines) to techniques of defence (such as taking self-defence classes). But these can also become unfair and oppressive, such as when women are forced to change the way they dress or look to avoid risks.

In terms of the broader landscape of urban violence and conflicts in Maré, women often mention calculating their places of refuge when a conflict breaks out. Staying at home when possible, especially in a back room to escape stray bullets, is the most preferred practice, which also allows them to be present in case of a police invasion in order to protect male family members. On the other hand, the home can sometimes not be a safe place for women, leading them to find refuge from combined public and private space violence in neutral spaces like shops or in the homes of their (usually female) neighbours, friends, and relatives. It is important to stress that, far from random, these coping practices and strategies are learned and taught between women in the community and passed on from generations.

When it comes to resisting and fighting back against the violence of racist discrimination and territorial stigma, racialized women

Figure 1.2: 'We have the right to take care of ourselves'. Illustration based on a focus group with five women from Maré, Rio de Janeiro. Credit: Mila de Choch (McIlwaine, 2022a)

from Maré often affirm their conditions of *faveladas*, reappropriating this term for themselves and using it in powerful personal narratives. When circulating in areas considered hostile, like affluent neighbourhoods and places frequented by cultural elites such as universities and theatres, they will make sure to speak up about their ancestry, community history, and heritage, aiming to provoke discomfort and gradually change racialized, classed, and gendered narratives about their community. (See Figure 1.2 which summarizes many aspects of women's everyday resistance practices in Maré including self-care, engaging with NGOs such as Casa das Mulheres, and education.)

Women in Maré are speaking up as part of a wider chain of voices that women are weaving everywhere to respond, resist, and counter everyday forms of gendered and intersectional violence. In India, for example, the organization Safetipin has been successful in raising awareness gender-based violence in the streets, responding with a range of mobile phone applications that feed into strategic urban planning. These ideas and initiatives have spread to Colombia, where similar forms of tactical knowledge influence the management of gendered urban violence in the public sphere (see Box 1.2 above).

Resisting gendered urban violence through longer-term initiatives

Throughout Latin America, a prolific variety of creative, longer-term, and transformative initiatives to resist gendered violence has emerged over the last few decades. In Latin American cities, community-based organizations, women-led resistance practices, and articulated social struggles have historically flourished in poor urban communities, especially around community improvements in relation to housing tenure, basic services, and public security. Longer-term initiatives of resistance include women returning to school, getting professional training, and improving their employability – in order to achieve greater financial autonomy, to break cycles of violence at home, and to be able to improve their living conditions away from violent urban areas. Women throughout the region also engage with other women in associations, religious groups, feminist collectives, support networks, and social projects.

These kinds of collective engagements can be life-changing, as they allow women to share coping mechanisms and tactical survival knowledge between each other, helping women to reassess their ongoing painful experiences as *violence* and empowering them to take action against it. This is because, although most women are aware of what constitutes gender-based violence, many can be less aware that psychological and financial abuse constitutes a form of violence until they learn from other women's experiences or visit a women's organization in search of other forms of support.

All these processes occur in Maré in Rio de Janeiro. Organizations that support women, although they are not part of the formal state network of protection and care, often have a high level of institutionalization and offer long-standing services in the community. In the absence of public services, these organizations form an important (and often the only) support network for women. Casa das Mulheres da Maré, which is a branch of Redes da Maré, a key organization in the neighbourhood, challenges gender-based violence through various projects to support women (see above).

Casa das Mulheres da Maré is always keen to address the entire spectrum of women's intersectional experiences. For example, they have been expanding their work with trans women in recent years and have also renovated their building to make it accessible so that they can begin to work with disabled women.

A part of their diverse range of services and projects, as the Casa's coordinator Julia Leal describes in our podcast series (2022), is an understanding that 'isolated actions are not enough to tackle the complex demands the women have':

> 'The idea is that a woman who arrives at the Women's House has access to a whole range of options to tap into. Therefore, a woman might arrive here spontaneously asking to speak with a lawyer, and be sent to take a course, because we recognize that she is being subjected to violence and understand that the experience of being with other women and hearing their stories could be strengthening for this woman.

> 'All of our courses are offered alongside classes in Gender Studies. This is part of the basic curriculum of any course we offer, they are obligatory classes. Therefore, this is also a space for political formation, in which we talk about gender, sexuality, race, body, territory. These classes become times of exchange, to which women bring their own experience.'

At Casa das Mulheres, women are supported to undertake transformative processes with autonomy. With expert guidance, they choose the resources they will use, including professional training, support groups, legal advice, adult education, entrepreneurship, and cooperative work. The outcomes of this tend to be extremely positive. Michele Gandra, a beneficiary who became a cook at the cooperative cooking project *Maré de Sabores,* highlights this in the podcast:

> 'It was there that I recognized myself as a woman who was going through things that other women were going through too... It was there that we found a refuge with one another. It was there that we came to understand the multiple forms of violence in the world. We spoke a lot about other countries too, how women are treated in other countries, different cultures and all that.

> And it was then that I started to see, to notice violence. I consider myself a privileged woman. I've been married for 28 years... But there was the first hurdle, of that person who understands, who begins to confront things.

> And now, the transformation... Because I'm not the only one who's transformed. I transform myself. I transform my partner. I transform my children. I transform and I'm transformed the whole time. My in-laws, my relationship with the neighbourhood.'

Michele's experience shows how the Casa das Mulheres and the women who work and are beneficiaries there are fundamental to social change, and that the organization provides a space for women's resistance to emerge. This is especially important for Black women, as Julia notes in the podcast:

'I understand that women, particularly Black women, are the cogs that keep Brazilian society going. I think they are the people who work most to begin with... If Black women in Brazil are the ones who suffer the most from gender-based violence, it is these women that have to be there drawing up public policy, instead of the way it is currently being done, which is half a dozen white men in a room producing country laws.'

Women in Maré are a force to be reckoned with as they challenge gendered violence through informal and formal means. What's more, many women are also engaged in resistance through various art forms as they 'conquer their spaces'. A recent online exhibition ('Vidas Femininas') with the Museu da Pessoa (Museum of the Person) showcases the stories of 10 women from Maré who have addressed gendered urban violence through music, dance, poetry, and other art forms. Their stories highlight how art can be a form of self-care, protest, self-affirmation, and above all, power, in allowing them to speak and to resist.[6]

Organizations like Casa das Mulheres in Maré exist throughout Latin America. Indeed, there are hundreds of 'women's houses' across cities in Latin America, most of which provide support for women survivors of gendered violence. For example, in Santa Cruz in Bolivia, the Casa de la Mujer provides an emergency refuge and both legal and psychological assistance for women fleeing gender-based violence (or what they call 'machista violence'), as well as providing workshops and running a radio station to raise awareness. While organizations like these tend to operate at the community level, others focus on advocacy and changing public policies. EQUIS Justicia para las Mujeres in Mexico, for example, works to transform institutions, laws, and public policies to improve access to justice for women.

COVID-19 and women's resistance

The intensification of gendered violence against women and girls during the COVID-19 pandemic has been widely reported in Latin America and indeed, globally. Due to lockdown measures in potentially unsafe homes and inability to work, women living on urban margins have been facing disproportionate struggles with illness, grief, and economic crisis, in addition to increases in domestic abuse. These conditions also brought severe challenges to pre-existing networks of support and daily coping practices amongst women facing intersectional inequalities, endemic urban violence, and state neglect. Yet, women across the world, and in Latin America specifically, have sought to respond to the pandemic by creating emergency responses to provide basic needs as well as assistance for those facing increased domestic violence. Various networks of mutual support, solidarity, and activism have been created locally and globally to address the critical challenges of the pandemic in relation to gendered violence in urban margins.[7]

In Mexico on International Women's Day 2020, around 80,000 women took to the streets to protest and start a national strike against gendered violence and the national femicide epidemic. This reflected the growing strength of women's collectives in the city (with more than 100 emerging) but also the onset of the COVID-19 pandemic and the related rise in domestic violence and especially femicides (939 cases between 2020 and 2021 and an increase of 130 per cent between 2015-2020) (Soloman, Martinez & Diaz, 2021). However, there is evidence that these feminist collectives have strengthened during the pandemic in relation to raising awareness of domestic violence as well as food security – often, but not exclusively through social media and online platforms. For example, the feminist collective Cruces X Rosas created a video to raise awareness of violence in quarantine and another, Brujas Feministas, established feminist barter-trading on social media platforms where women could exchange services and products and find community in the face of COVID-19 (Ventura Alfaro, 2020).

Similar processes occurred in Maré. The first was a women-led grassroots campaign to address urgent basic needs by distributing food and hygiene goods. The campaign Maré Says No to Coronavirus (*Campanha Maré Diz Não ao Coronavírus*) started in March 2020 focusing on six areas: food security; assistance to the homeless; income generation; access to health rights, care, and prevention; production and dissemination of secure information; support for local artists and cultural groups. The distribution of basic food baskets and personal hygiene items was organized according to various criteria of social vulnerability. Between March and December 2020, items were delivered to over 17,500 families, directly benefiting almost 55,000 people – mainly female heads of household (79 per cent). The activities were led and delivered by women, including 54 seamstresses sewing facemasks and 22 cooks preparing daily meals for free distribution for those who were self-isolating (13 men were also involved as drivers to deliver donations).[8] Gradually, the campaign took on a rights and healthcare structure. They developed an online service to log cases of violence and violations of rights, to monitor COVID-19 cases, and to organize support in accessing medical treatments, mass testing, and telemedicine services. The emergency response transformed into a more multifaceted initiative and the organization went on to create a communication channel for women to discuss self-care and reproductive and mental health with the Casa das Mulheres. Some of the topics covered were reproductive rights, livelihoods, professional training, adult and early childhood education, school registration, and persisting armed violence and police brutality.

The second women-led initiative Support Network for Women in Maré (RAMM - Rede de Apoio às Mulheres da Maré) was initiated in May 2020 by the organization Fight for Peace (*Luta Pela Paz*), to deal with the rise in domestic violence during the lockdown measures in the overcrowded homes of Maré. RAMM realized that with better coordination, professionals in different areas of care could be unified in order to build joint strategies linking public policy arenas, local civil society organizations, and academic researchers. RAMM's first action was to construct an 'integrated workflow' for 40 collaborating institutions who were supporting women in Maré. The workflow was created through a participatory process which included mapping services, policies, and meetings with representatives around solidarity, and noting the urgent need to address domestic violence. Once completed, the workflow was disseminated through public events and online strategies. There was a clear transition from the campaign's initial reactive responses to more strategic activities, when RAMM began not only providing service information but also offering training for social workers and community members assisting women survivors of gendered violence. The programme 'Capacity-building in assistance to women in Maré' was developed in early 2021 and aimed to develop longer-term strategies for addressing gendered and intersectional urban violence in Maré.

In the face of endemic urban gendered violence, these processes are gradual and often fragmented, yet a feminist potency surged from the crisis, and it has been used to improve the lives of women in Maré and elsewhere (see Box 1.3 on emotional-political communities).

Box 1.3: Building emotional-political communities in Maré during COVID-19

Latin American feminist debates traditionally highlight organized and collaborative practices to confront gendered violence against women, particularly in high-conflict urban areas. They emphasize how these practices may become more political and strategic over time, as women further develop consciousness of their gendered and intersectional oppressions. Taking the lead from Colombian anthropologist, Myriam Jimeno, it has been shown that when survivors of violence in Latin America share personal testimonies, emotional bonds are created which may be reconfigured into political action and 'emotional-political communities' (Jimeno, 2010).

Such 'emotional-political communities' have been built in Maré during times of COVID-19 as part of resistance efforts to deal with both the pandemic and gendered urban violence. Women's collective emergency responses to the crisis have inspired further awakening among other women survivors of gendered violence. 'Emotional-political communities' are reactive in responding to immediate crises and providing momentary solutions – offering sustenance, shelter, basic information, and expert advice. They also become transformative over time, providing economic opportunities to women and encouraging them to organize around reproductive rights and other social justice issues in the context of wider urban and structural violence. This fosters societal change, collectively.

Women-led initiatives can therefore help other women to deal with the severe care and livelihood burdens of the pandemic, gradually leading to more initiatives to foster autonomy and prevent of gendered violence, especially among Black women. Michele Gandra from the cooperative cooking project in Casa das Mulheres spoke of her personal journey of building social and gendered consciousness after joining:

'We don't change from outside in; we change from inside out. The seed I plant here in my home I hope that it multiplies, among my neighbours, among my community. This is how we try to change. Change for the better.'

Source: McIlwaine et al. (2022b)

This chapter has shown how women in Latin America are far from passive in the face of burgeoning urban violence and conflict, which has been exacerbated by the onset of the COVID-19 pandemic alongside increases in domestic violence and femicide. The discussion has been rooted in ongoing research and drawing from one of our podcasts in the favela communities of Maré in Rio de Janeiro as well as from examples from other parts of the region. It has attempted to show the potency of women's responses as they have developed short and long-term resistance practices, both informal formal. Just as gendered urban violence is experienced in intersectional, direct, and indirect ways -which in the case of Maré shows how poor Black women suffer disproportionately - women's coping mechanisms and resistance strategies are also varied. The chapter has also highlighted initiatives from Colombia that work to create safer cities and from Mexico, where feminist collectives have responded positively to the pandemic. In Brazil's Maré, we have shown how 'emotional-political communities' have been built. It is fitting to end the chapter with the Mexican proverb mobilized in the wake of the murder of Marielle Franco: they wanted to bury us, but they didn't know we were seeds.

Notes

1.   Gendered intersectional violence against women and girls refers to direct or indirect violence perpetrated on grounds of gender, race,

ethnicity, class, sexuality, age, disability and/or any other form of discrimination.

2. Casa das Mulheres (Women's House) was established in 2016 by Redes da Maré and forms part of the organization's women and gender pillar. Its aim is to foster the role of women in the favelas and improve their lives and living conditions. See more at McIlwaine (2021b).

3. See Wright (2021).

4. This chapter draws on research collaborations through two projects directed by McIlwaine: Transnational VAWG (2016-2019) and Dignity and Resilience (2019-2021).The first is funded by the ESRC (ES/N013247/1) and the second by the British Academy and the Global Challenges Research Fund (HDV190030).

5. Smith (2018) places these experiences within a wider context of gendered 'necropolitics', a term was coined by Achille Mbembe which refers to how states decide which lives are more valuable than others. See https://criticallegalthinking.com/2020/03/02/achille-mbembe-necropolitics.

6. Access the online exhibition at https://vidasfemininas.museudapessoa.org/

7. See examples of women's mobilizations here: https://lac.unwomen.org/en/noticias-y-eventos/articulos/2020/11/impacto-economico-covid-19-mujeres-america-latina-y-el-caribe.

8. See *Redes da Maré*'s 2020 report on the campaign's outcomes at: https://www.redesdamare.org.br/media/downloads/arquivos/RdM_Relatorio_campanha.pdf.

Bibliography

Carneiro, S. (2003) 'Mulheres em movimento', *Estudos Avançados*, 17(49)

Félix de Souza, N.M. and Rodrigues Selis, L.M. (2022) 'Gender violence and feminist resistance in Latin America', *International Feminist Journal of Politics*, 24(1), pp. 5-15

Garayo Willemyns, J. (2021) 'A sunflower in her hair', *Latin America Bureau*, 7 April, https://lab.org.uk/a-sunflower-in-her-hair

House, D. (2015) 'Mexico: the politics of memory', *Latin America Bureau*, 9 February, https://lab.org.uk/mexico-the-politics-of-memory

Jimeno, M. (2010) 'Emoções e política: a vítima e a construção de comunidades emocionais', *Mana* 16(1), pp. 99-121

Loureiro, G.S. (2020) 'To be black, queer and radical: centring the epistemology of Marielle Franco', *Open Cultural Studies* 4, pp. 50-58, https://doi.org/10.1515/culture-2020-0005

McIlwaine, C. (2013) 'Urbanization and gender-based violence: exploring the paradoxes in the global south', *Environment and Urbanization* 25(1), pp. 65-79, https://doi.org/10.1177/0956247813477359

McIlwaine, C. (2021a) 'Gendered urban violence against women and girls from the margins to the centre', in: Amin, A. and Clarke, H. (eds.) *Urban Violence*. London: British Academy, pp. 27-31, https://www.thebritishacademy.ac.uk/documents/3340/Urban-Violence.pdf

McIlwaine, C (2021b) 'Organisations | Redes da Maré and Casa das Mulheres, Rio de Janeiro', *Latin America Bureau,* 30 July, https://lab.org.uk/wrv-organisations-redes-da-mare-casa-das-mulheres-rio

McIlwaine, C., Krenzinger, M., Evans, Y. and Sousa Silva, E. (2020) 'Feminised urban futures, healthy cities and Violence Against Women and Girls (VAWG)', in: Keith, M. and Aruska de Souza Santos, A. (eds.) *Urban transformations and public health in the emergent city.* Manchester: MUP Press, pp. 55-78, https://www.manchester-openhive.com/view/9781526150943/9781526150943.xml

McIlwaine, C., Krenzinger, M., Rizzini Ansari, M., Evans, Y. and Sousa Silva, E. (2021) 'O direito à cidade de mulheres: uma análise sobre suas limitações a partir de violências infraestruturais de gênero contra brasileiras em Londres e na Maré, Rio de Janeiro', *Revista de Direito da Cidade* 13(2), pp. 954-981, https://kclpure.kcl.ac.uk/portal/files/154309041/Published_Paper_Revista_Direito_da_Cidade_Vol_13_n_2_2021.pdf

McIlwaine, C., Coelho Resende, N., Rizzini Ansari, M., Dionisio, A., Gonçalves Leal, J., Vieira, F., Krenzinger, M., Heritage, P., Peppl, R. and Sousa Silva, E. (2022a) 'Resistance practices to address gendered urban violence in Maré, Rio de Janeiro', https://drive.google.com/file/d/1i7CJL5jOdwfU3r-q0d0eOiO0YWz-CaBY/view

McIlwaine, C., Krenzinger, M., Rizzini Ansari, M., Coelho Resende, N., Gonçalves Leal, J. and Vieira, F. (2022b) 'Building emotional political communities to address gendered violence against women and girls during COVID-19 in the favelas of Maré, Rio de Janeiro', *Social and Cultural Geography*, https://doi.org/10.1080/14649365.2022.2065697

Krenzinger, M., Sousa Silva, E., McIlwaine, C. and Heritage, P. (eds.) (2018) *Dores que libertam: falas de mulheres das favelas da Maré, no Rio de Janeiro, sobre violências.* Rio de Janeiro: Appris Editora

Krenzinger, M., Farias, P., Morgado, R. and McIlwaine, C. (2021) 'Violência de gênero e desigualdade racial em uma pesquisa com mulheres no território conflagrado do conjunto de favelas da Maré/Rio de Janeiro', *Revista Trabalho Necessario* 19(38), pp. 266-289, https://periodicos.uff.br/trabalhonecessario/article/view/47366

Pain, R. (2014) 'Seismologies of emotion: fear and activism during domestic violence', *Social & Cultural Geography* 15(2), pp. 127-150, https://doi.org/10.1080/14649365.2013.862846

Perry, K-K. Y. (2013) *Black women against the land grab.* Minneapolis: University of Minnesota Press.

Rocha, J. (2018) 'The four bullets that killed Marielle', *Latin America Bureau,* 23 March, https://lab.org.uk/the-four-bullets-that-killed-marielle

Smith, C.A. (2017) 'Battling anti-black genocide in Brazil', *NACLA Report on the Americas* 49(1), pp. 41–47, https://doi.org/10.1080/10714839.2017.1298243

Smith, C.A. (2018) 'Lingering trauma in Brazil', *NACLA Report on the Americas,* 27 December, https://nacla.org/news/2019/01/02/lingering-trauma-brazil-police-violence-against-black-women

Solomon, D.B., Martinez, A.I. and Diaz, L. (2021) 'Women march in Mexico to make their voices heard, seek justice', *Reuters,* 8 March, https://www.reuters.com/article/us-womens-day-mexico-march-idUSKBN2B02CO

UN Women (2017) 'Safe cities and safe public spaces initiative', Global results report, https://www.unwomen.org/en/digital-library/publications/2017/10/safe-cities-and-safe-public-spaces-globalresults-report

Ventura Alfaro, M. J. (2020) 'Feminist solidarity networks have multiplied since the COVID-19 outbreak in Mexico', *Interface* 12(1), pp. 82–87, https://www.interfacejournal.net/wp-content/uploads/2020/05/Ventura-Alfaro-1.pdf

Viswanath, K. and Basu, A. (2015) 'SafetiPin: an innovative mobile app to collect data on women's safety in Indian cities', *Gender & Development* 23(1), pp. 45–60, https://doi.org/10.1080/13552074.2015.1013669.

WHO (2018) 'Violence against women prevalence estimates, 2018 – global fact sheet', https://www.who.int/publications/i/item/WHO-SRH-21.6

Wright, A (2021) 'Understanding violence against women and girls in Brazil'. *Latin America Bureau,* 24 September, https://lab.org.uk/understanding-violence-against-women-and-girls-in-brazil

CHAPTER 2

'*Care for those who care*': Domestic workers fight back against violence

Marilyn Thomson

> 'Violence against domestic workers ranges from the disrespectful way employers speak to us – being shouted at and insulted – to not having our labour rights. Considering all the different forms of violence that affect domestic workers gives a broader understanding of our needs as workers.' (Ana Laura Aquino, 2021)

The home should be a place of safety, a haven for rest and recuperation, but all too often it is a site of violence and abuse. Intimate partner violence is reported by UN Women as the most prevalent form of VAWG globally, and one of the greatest human rights violations, which increased alarmingly during the COVID-19 pandemic (Mlambo-Ngcuka, 2020). Perhaps less often acknowledged is that violence in the home also impacts women employed to do the housework and to help with the care and wellbeing of family members. This chapter presents the intersecting forms of violence affecting women working in the sector. It highlights how, in recent years, domestic workers throughout Latin America have become empowered to speak out against their maltreatment by employers and as a result have become more visible as advocates for their rights as workers. The chapter features some of the achievements of domestic workers' organizations in resisting violence and discrimination against them in their workplace. It also gives an account of the transformation of domestic workers into activists defending their rights, nationally and regionally, and becoming players in the international policy arena.

In Latin America it is common practice for better-off families to employ one or even several household workers to help with the maintenance of the home and caring responsibilities. The International Labour Organisation (ILO) estimates there are between 11-18 million domestic workers in Latin America. The exact number is difficult to measure because it is often an invisible workforce, mainly working in the informal sector without rights to social security, medical care, pensions, and decent wages. Furthermore, ECLAC data indicates that Afro-descendant and Indigenous populations are over-represented in the sector (UN Women/ILO/ECLAC, 2020).

Domestic work is a very feminized occupation In Latin America given over 90 per cent of domestic workers are women and, due to the traditional gender division of labour, men employed in private homes have more valued jobs as chauffeurs or gardeners and often receive better pay than women working within the household. Care work within the family is usually considered to be the responsibility of low-paid women labourers, who carry out a wide range of supporting housekeeping tasks such as cleaning, washing and ironing clothes, buying and cooking food, and more responsible tasks like looking after children, the elderly, disabled people, and pets. The work is often mundane, repetitive, and regarded as unskilled – so not valued by society. There is also a social class division of roles, as the female employer supervises the work and delegates the tasks, rather than engaging in housework herself and can also enjoy greater leisure time. Many upper, middle class, and professional women can further their careers and engage in activities outside the home because they employ domestic workers, who are from a poorer social class, to carry out the domestic and caring responsibilities within the family.

Intersection of social class, ethnicity, race, and gender

Historically in Latin America, domestic service was a relationship between social classes akin to slavery, in which discrimination based on gender was compounded by racial and ethnic discrimination (UN Women/ILO/ECLAC, 2020). In the colonial period, servants were Afro-descendent, Indigenous, and mixed-raced people and today, although the nature of the job has changed, domestic work continues to be a sector where power relations and social inequalities prevail. Social class, ethnicity, and race – as well as gender – define this labour relationship, where women from the poorest, most marginalized groups in society wait on, serve, and clean up after the middle and upper classes. In Mexico, for example, it is estimated that one in five live-in domestic workers come from an Indigenous community and are migrants from rural areas, who might not speak Spanish fluently and often have low levels of formal education (CACEH, n/d).

Racism and cultural perceptions of household workers as servants or *muchachas* (little maids) persist in soap operas, magazines, and in social attitudes throughout Latin America. There are many stereotypes, some with racist overtones, that household workers are uneducated, ignorant, and 'loose women'. However, in recent years, several films have been produced in Latin America which are sympathetic to the situation of women domestic workers. The main protagonists in these films are domestic workers and the story is told from their perspective, depicting the social inequalities that exist in the relationships with family members. In films such as *La Nana* (Chile), and *Que horas ela volta?* (Brazil), the filmmakers show domestic workers standing up for themselves and responding to the maternalism and the inequality they face as they negotiate with their employers (Moynihan, 2020).

Child labour

The ILO estimates that around 2 million girls under 14 years old are engaged in domestic work throughout Latin America and are vulnerable to sexual harassment and other forms of physical abuse in the workplace. There are many reasons for this form of child labour, such as family breakups or children becoming orphans with no one to care for them. There are limited employment options for girls with little schooling, especially girls from Indigenous groups living in remote rural areas. It is still the case that employers go to villages and make informal agreements with parents of adolescent girls offering board, lodgings, and education in return for light housework - which is seldom the reality for these girls once they move to the city. In Peru, for example it is common practice for poor Indigenous families in rural areas to send their daughters to the city to stay with relatives to help with housework and continue their education at night school. There are also cases of girls fleeing family violence travelling on their own to cities and being taken in by 'godmothers'. These girls are not regarded as workers but as 'one of the family' and thus invisible to the authorities.

In a report on domestic child labour the ILO identified some of the most common risks child domestic workers face: long and tiring working days; use of toxic chemicals; carrying heavy loads; handling dangerous items such as knives, axes, and hot pans; insufficient or inadequate food and accommodation, and humiliating treatment including physical and verbal violence and sexual abuse. These hazards are compounded by the denial of the fundamental rights of the child, such as access to education and health care; the right to rest, leisure, play and recreation; and the right to have regular contact with their parents and peers. These factors can have an irreversible physical, psychological, and moral impact on the development, health, and wellbeing of a child (ILO, 2013).

Box 2.1: Ana Laura Aquino's Story

Although my parents are from Oaxaca, I don't identify as an Indigenous woman. I was born in Mexico City, and I don't speak an Indigenous language. Yes, I do have Indigenous roots, but I'm from the city. There are many stereotypes around domestic workers. They label us, they say that only poor, Indigenous women are doing this sort of work. But I think now it's more about different social classes than ethnicity.

I'm 46 years old and have been involved in domestic work since I was 13. This was forced child labour, necessary for us to survive. My mother was on her own and I had younger brothers and sisters who depended on her. She was a seamstress, and it wasn't easy to make ends meet with so many children. When she met a new partner and fell pregnant, she told me that if I wanted to carry on at school, I would need to become a live-in domestic worker. So that's how I began working. I started my chores at six in the morning working until around 1pm and then went to secondary school in the afternoons and evenings. Nowadays I work for two employers as well as working in an organization of domestic workers. I went back to secondary school recently and started studying again. Domestic work gives me flexibility and because I am not living-in I have time to do things for myself. It helps that I don't have children to support.

I have been organized for the past 19 years and I know my rights, which makes a difference as I can negotiate with employers. There are still many young girls coming from rural villages to the city who have no idea about their rights. There are also many employers who don't know that domestic workers have labour rights and because it is informal, they don't think it is a recognized occupation.

Source: Aquino (2021)

Violence against domestic workers

The nature of household employment in Latin America has changed in recent decades as more domestic workers gain greater knowledge of their rights because of the awareness-raising activities of domestic workers' organizations over many years. There are now more workers employed on a live-out basis, some working part-time or by the day with several employers. However, domestic work continues to be precarious and unregulated employment, with low wages, labour exploitation and abuse. It is difficult to protect the workers because the workplace is a private home. Employers often see themselves as benefactors offering charity by giving a poor woman a job. Even when labour rights exist on the statutes, these are difficult to enforce as there are no official mechanisms to report labour abuses.

'The issue of violence is one of the problems faced by domestic workers and they need to recognize different forms and how to respond. That's why we produced this poster, as these are the most common forms of violence. But we have identified 15 different types of violence they experience. But it is good that they now recognize these actions as violence.' (Marcelina Bautista, 2022)

A study carried out by international NGO CARE with members of the Latin American Confederation of Household Workers (CONLACTRAHO) examined workplace violence and abuse experienced by domestic workers in Ecuador, Colombia, México, Honduras, and Guatemala. In their survey with workers, they found that 8 out of 10 women employed in private households had experienced violence at work. This was a participatory study that identified common issues among domestic workers in all these countries relating to vulnerabilities, low status, and lack of employment rights. In a mapping exercise with a group of domestic workers in San Pedro Sula, Honduras, the women defined their experiences of violence in the workplace, as the following:

- Verbal abuse
- Sexual abuse and harassment
- Intimidation and psychological abuse
- Long working hours
- Low wages
- Threat of losing our jobs
- Lack of value given to our work
- Racism
- Discrimination.

Almost all of the women who participated in the CARE study were survivors of some form of violence in their workplace, exacerbated by the racism and machismo that prevail in society more generally. In the same study, participants in focus group discussions in other countries further identified violence as: economic and labour exploitation, loss of freedom, deception, and control by withholding passports of migrant workers. The study also found that sexual harassment and abuse against domestic workers intensified in the case of Afro-descendant women, who were hyper-sexualized by male employers. Some workers reported they had tried to put a stop to harassment by telling their female employer about their spouses but were not believed or were accused of provoking the situation. In a mapping exercise with a group in Ecuador, participants were asked where they felt safe within the home. Many participants identified the master's bedroom as a place to be feared: 'We know that in the employers' bedrooms many women became pregnant after being raped there'. They also confirmed that in their experiences, 'Afro-Ecuadorians and Indigenous women are the most exploited, but it's harder on Indigenous women because their culture doesn't allow them to talk about the abuse' (CARE, 2018).

There are of course many good employers, but there are also bad employers, and the ill-treatment is often by the female employer and even by children in the family. Many employers are not aware that they have legal responsibilities and domestic workers' organizations are attempting to change this. They provide information to employers about the labour rights of domestic workers and negotiate with them to provide proper employment contracts. The tide is beginning to turn as domestic workers in Latin America are organized, supporting each other, and campaigning against violence and harassment in the workplace which will be featured later in this chapter.

> 'Employers think they are doing us a favour; they don't value our work and they don't know that we have labour rights.' (Ana Laura Aquino, 2021)

Domestic workers impacted by COVID-19

The COVID-19 pandemic has unveiled many social inequalities globally and has had the greatest impact on the most vulnerable, especially women working in the informal sector and low-paid caring jobs. Within the domestic employment sector, the pandemic exacerbated an already precarious situation, exposed many injustices, violence, maltreatment, and exploitation. In response to reports from member organizations during the pandemic, the International Domestic Workers' Federation (IDWF) and 29 domestic workers' unions and organizations from 15 Latin American countries collaborated with the ILO to produce guidance for domestic workers and their employers. This guidance highlighted the poor occupational health and safety conditions faced by domestic workers which were accentuated during the pandemic. Some of the risk factors identified were: long working hours without rest periods; isolation; night shifts; physical, psychological, and emotional overload; lack of recognition of their work; monotonous and repetitive tasks; unfair, discriminatory, and threatening treatment. The guidelines stress that these working conditions have negative impacts on the physical and mental health of domestic workers leading to stress, anxiety, psychological disorders, fatigue, and emotional exhaustion (ILO, 2022).

During the pandemic, domestic workers were disproportionately impacted by unemployment, or alternatively an intensification of tasks, and they often lacked legal and social protection to help mitigate the effects of the COVID-19 crisis (UN Women/ILO/ECLAC, 2020). An IDWF report, based on surveys of live-in domestic workers across the Americas, found that psychological, physical, and sexual violence increased during the pandemic and that domestic workers were exposed to greater sexual harassment from male employers who were working from home (IDWF/FITH, 2020).

In our interview, Ana Laura spoke about a recent virtual forum she had participated in with other organized domestic workers from Latin American and the Caribbean (held in October 2021) to discuss the impact of the pandemic on the sector. They identified similar experiences in all countries where there were massive dismissals of domestic workers without severance pay or in other cases salaries were cut and working hours increased and overall workers' rights were not respected. Some workers were forbidden by employers to return to their own homes at night if they wanted to keep their jobs. Others who travelled on public transport to get to work had to pay for their own protective masks and gloves out of their meagre wages. Some of the women who were laid off without pay had to sell belongings to pay their rent, to eat, and to feed their children. Several gave away their pets because they could not afford to feed them. Others were forced into the informal sector, for example preparing and selling food in the street, which increased their vulnerability to infection. In desperation, those with no income returned to their home villages to stay with family members, which often led to family violence in overcrowded homes.

> 'Employers were indifferent to the financial and emotional situation of their workers. Many workers were locked in and were prohibited from seeing their relatives who were ill or from going to family funerals. When employers got back in touch with workers they had laid off, they didn't offer any back pay or compensation for the time they had been laid off, and even cut their wages, saying they couldn't afford to pay them more.' (Ana Laura Aquino, 2021)

Organizations of domestic workers responded to the pandemic through a regional campaign called Care for Those Who Care (#CuidaAQuienTeCuida). It was launched initially by trade unions of domestic workers in Mexico, Argentina, Brazil, and Chile and then spread throughout the continent on social media. The campaign raised awareness of the exposure of domestic workers to the virus, including in quarantine, and informed them of protective measures to take if they continued working during the pandemic. In Mexico, the campaign was run by CACEH (Centre for Professional Training and Leadership for Household Workers) and they won support from artists and film producers who joined their efforts to raise awareness among employers about the rights of domestic workers (see 'Inspirational leaders changing perceptions', this chapter). Using social media, the campaign urged workers and their employers to sign a written contract that stipulates working hours, tasks, holidays, and wages.[1]

Figure. 2.1: Care for Those Who Care campaign poster. Credit: Contagio de Conscienca/ Facebook

Migration and domestic work

Poverty and social conflicts are the main drivers for migration of families from rural areas to the cities and from poorer countries to wealthier ones within Latin America, and ultimately to the US and Europe in the search for a better life. According to the ILO, up to 60 per cent of internal and transborder female migrants are working in the domestic work sector (UN Women/ILO/ECLAC, 2020). Disaggregated data on migration and ethnicity or race is very limited, and the ILO has recently started conducting country studies to further investigate the specific situation of Indigenous domestic workers.[2] Throughout Latin America it is common for Indigenous and Afro-descendent women from rural and coastal villages to migrate to towns and cities in search of work and better opportunities. Live-in domestic work is often the best option for single women migrants as it gives them somewhere to live, but it can also expose them to greater labour exploitation and abuse, and their status as migrants makes them vulnerable to discrimination and violence.

According to the IDWF, during the COVID-19 pandemic migrant women have been disproportionately impacted by job losses and layoffs in the cleaning and domestic work sectors throughout the continent. This has led to increased economic insecurity, which is a risk factor for gender-based violence and harassment because workers are more dependent on their jobs and less able to report abusive behaviour by their employers (IDWF/FITH, 2020).

In the UK there is a significant Latin American community who came to the country as migrants and refugees – currently the largest national groups are from Brazil, Colombia, Peru, and Ecuador (see Chapter 5). Initially, many face problems getting employment because they don't speak English and do not know the system or culture, and so they are forced into precarious and informal jobs such as domestic work, office cleaning, hospitality, and catering. Even middle-class, qualified migrants (both men and women) work in the cleaning sector because language barriers make it difficult to apply for other types of jobs when they first arrive. Recent changes in UK immigration visa requirements do not recognize domestic work and cleaning as valid employment for migrant workers, which has led to some migrant women becoming undocumented and more vulnerable to labour exploitation. In addition, the government's 'hostile environment' toward migrants makes it difficult for women workers to report harassment and maltreatment in the workplace for fear of deportation.

The Latin American Women's Rights Service (LAWRS)[3] carried out research with 326 women who were supported by their employment rights advice service, to investigate labour rights violations experienced by migrant women employed in cleaning, hospitality, and domestic work. Over 40 per cent of the women interviewed had experienced discrimination, harassment, or unreasonable treatment in the workplace and reported labour exploitation (such as long working hours and low pay) as well as health and safety issues. There were 11 cases of potential trafficking for labour exploitation, seven were cleaners or hospitality workers and four were domestic workers. Responses from 52 domestic workers in the survey found that 57 per cent experienced verbal abuse and threats and 14 per cent experienced physical abuse and/or sexual harassment (Da Silva, 2019).

Not all migrant workers are treated badly but a significant number are, and therefore actions are needed to identify, document cases, and protect migrant women from maltreatment and labour exploitation, as shown in this same research report. Leticia, from Bolivia, explains:

'You can't even get help because they threaten you and you don't speak English, so what are you going to do? Be homeless? You stay and they keep abusing you, and there is nothing you can do.' (Da Silva, 2019: 10)

Alicia, from Mexico, adds:

'Being a domestic worker is dangerous, your bosses almost own you. They brought you to the country, so you feel like you owe them, but they treat you like a slave. You work as a cleaner, cook, nanny, receptionist, you do it all...' (Da Silva, 2019: 8)

As part of their Community Activism programme, LAWRS collaborated with the City of London Corporation in 2018 with an awareness-raising campaign on domestic abuse. Building on its success, in 2019 LAWRS was approached again by the corporation to work together on a new campaign on harassment in the workplace. They organized two focus groups with Latin American migrant women working as office cleaners to identify issues for the new campaign on the hidden workforce in the city being planned for 2020. Participants contributed ideas on how to address harassment, abuse, and exploitation of cleaners as the campaign aimed to target employers and demand account-ability to tackle the issue of sexual harassment in the workplace. Unfortunately, due to the pandemic, the campaign was postponed but it is a good indicator of the success of LAWRS' advocacy strategy in reaching policy and decision-makers to take preventive actions and make the situation of migrant workers more visible. During the pandemic, LAWRS was forced to close its drop-in advice service but provided a helpline instead. Advice on their webpage covers many critical issues such as how to deal with domestic violence and how to identify, prevent, and take actions on harassment in the workplace.

Domestic workers organizing for change

The Latin American Confederation of Household Workers (CONLACTRAHO) was founded in March 1988 at the first regional meeting of domestic workers which was held in Bogota, Colombia, bringing together participants from 11 countries. Despite political and cultural differences between their countries, they found many commonalities in their labour situation, the discrimination and racism they faced, and their vulnerabilities as workers. The founders of the

Confederation were clear in defining their aims: to win and defend their labour rights, and for domestic workers to become aware that they have these rights. So, they developed a platform for action that continues to this day. Fundamental to their ethos is that domestic workers must be the protagonists of their own struggle and not submit to the decisions of others – be it employers, academics, trade unionists, or other women's organizations – and that their affiliates should be autonomous domestic workers' organizations led by domestic workers (Goldsmith, 2013).

Since then and with scant resources, CONLACTRAHO has mobilized and pushed for legislation and labour reforms at national and international levels to support the rights of workers employed in private households. CONLACTRHO is a member of the IDWF and with them began lobbying for legislation to protect the rights of domestic workers through an international campaign calling for decent work for domestic workers in 2009.[4] CONLACTRAHO took this campaign forward in Latin America and the Caribbean. The demands of IDWF were put on the agenda of the ILO at two conferences in 2010 and 2011, where domestic workers represented themselves in negotiations with the ILO. This was the first time that the workers directly affected by an international instrument participated in an ILO conference, as previously others have spoken and decided on their behalf, and it was immensely symbolic that they were physically present at the events. As Mary Goldsmith points out (2013), their active participation also proved to be empowering for the delegates and brought into play the redistribution of power, recognition, and representation of domestic workers. Years of advocacy and negotiations by the sector were finally successful when the ILO published the International Convention on Decent Work for Domestic Workers (C189) in 2011, which was drawn up with the input of representatives of IDWF from around the world.

Today, CONLACTRAHO has among its affiliates a variety of household workers' organizations in 14 Latin American countries, as well as the US and Canada. Some are larger and better funded than others, some are legally recognized trade unions, others are federations or associations with not-for-profit status, and others are looser networks. CONLACTRAHO provides technical support to help members grow and amplify their voices in decision-making spaces. In recent years, they have implemented projects to support member organizations in the region through an initiative called Equal Value, Equal Rights (with support from CARE international and others) which has had many positive results in the participating countries (Colombia, Ecuador, Guatemala, Honduras, Brazil, and México).

There is a long history of women workers in this sector organizing to fight for their rights throughout the continent, and several interesting examples of activities undertaken by domestic workers' organizations to mitigate violence. Some of these organizations have taken an intersectional approach to address the social and labour conditions of Black and Indigenous women in the labour market. For example, in Colombia, the Union of Afro-Colombian Workers in Domestic Service (UTRASD) was founded in Medellin in March 2013 following a meeting of 28 Afro-descendent women.[5] There is a large Black population in the city and few other employment opportunities for women from these communities apart from domestic work.

> 'We wanted to highlight the Afro [women] because as Black people, historically, we have suffered the greatest humiliations due to racism, socioeconomic status, low level of education, and immigration status. All these factors have contributed to the fact that the Black woman who works in a house is seen as worthless. People imagine that Black people are strong and therefore we must be exploited more severely.' (UTRASD, n/d)

UTRASD participated in a study carried out in Medellin on the conditions of Afro-descendant women, which highlights the vicious circle of racism and how it affects the rights of Black women migrants and those born in the city. They found that racial discrimination limits their access to higher education, the health service, and employment in the formal sector, so that domestic work becomes their only option for employment (CARE & Fundación Bien Humano, 2021). For live-in domestic workers, conditions are particularly difficult and can affect their mental health:

> '... as a trade union, we are raising our voices and raising awareness of our situation in society, so that the government, rather than pitying us, hear the truth about what harms us. By doing this, we want to help prevent injustices against domestic workers. Our lived experiences are what led us to organize to stop the exploitation and mistreatment of women, especially Afro women, which is very common. The Union is a meeting and solidarity space for workers who have little free time and other limitations... although we have advanced in our struggle, we are clear that there is still a long way to go.' (UTRASD, n/d)

Working on a larger scale in Brazil, the National Federation of Domestic Workers (FENATRAD) brings together 22 trade unions representing approximately 7.2 million domestic workers in 13 states. It grew out of an association created in 1936, and the organization was strengthened in 1972 with the passing of a law recognizing domestic work as an occupation rather than personal services. On their website FENATRAD points out that Black women in this sector are subjected to racial prejudice, as well as physical and sexual aggression. The Federation provides advice and orientation for members, and gives the following descriptions of harassment in the workplace to help women become more aware of these abuses and to report them:

> 'Moral harassment is all types of abusive behaviour that the employer exhibits in the workplace. If you are forced to work longer than required by law or are threatened with being fired all the time for no apparent reason, you may be the victim of harassment. Swearing, and exposure to repeated humiliations are also harassment.'

> 'Sexual harassment is characterized by indiscreet comments, whispers and innuendos that make you feel uncomfortable and that are practiced by people who are above you in the workplace. Demanding that you do some sexual favour in exchange for a job, or a pay rise is the best-known form.' (FENATRAD)

In Mexico, the Centre for Professional Training and Leadership for Household Workers (CACEH) was set up in 2000 as an autonomous space for domestic workers to come together to learn, share, and develop themselves professionally through technical and political training. The guidance they provide includes information on cultural identity and non-discrimination of Indigenous women working in domestic service:

> 'Indigenous women suffer double social discrimination, even in families and communities. As household workers they suffer even more, not only discrimination but also exploitation, maltreatment, labour abuse, and sexual abuse from their employers. This situation is not correct, not justified, not acceptable. It should not be allowed and should be punished according to the laws.' (CACEH, n/d)

CACEH supports women to become leaders who will promote and disseminate domestic workers' rights and their obligations within the community. An important recent innovation of CACEH was a free app for mobile phones called Dignas (translates to 'dignified') which is designed to help workers negotiate with their employers and ensure they receive their entitlements under existing labour legislation in Mexico. The app includes a summary of labour rights and a calculator which, for example, with inputs on salary and time spent in a job, can

Figure. 2.2: The Dignas mobile app. Credit: CACEH, Mexico

tell the worker the number of holiday days and annual bonus they are due, as well as the amount of compensation due if they are laid off. Marcelina Bautista from CACEH explains (2022): 'Dignas is a great digital tool which is helping workers calculate their labour rights. We are now updating it to include calculations for other labour rights.'

CACEH has jointly organized forums on rights and dignity at work with the Mexican Human Rights Commission, focusing on specific themes including discrimination and violence in the workplace. To reach out to more women, they often hold workshops in the parks where domestic workers usually congregate on Sundays, their day off. They also offer a range of training sessions on topics such as self-esteem and wellbeing, the social security system, health and safety at work, leadership, and violence against women in the workplace. During the pandemic the training courses moved online but they have recently re-started training sessions in person at various locations around the country.

Inspirational leaders changing perceptions

Marcelina Bautista, the director and founder of CACEH, is an Indigenous woman from Oaxaca who migrated to Mexico City at the age of 14 and was employed in domestic work. In her twenties she became involved in organising other domestic workers and in 2000 she set up CACEH. Marcelina was the General Secretary of CONLACTRAHO for several years and was involved in the drafting process of the ILO Domestic Workers Convention C189. Some of her many achievements include being awarded a prestigious prize for equality and non-discrimination from the Mayor of Mexico City and she has also won international recognition, receiving a human rights award from Friedrich Ebert Stiftung in Germany in 2010, and in 2021 was named as one of the BBC's 100 Inspirational Women. Marcelina was invited as guest of honour to the premiere of the 2018 Oscar-winning foreign language film, *Roma,* by the director Alfonso Cuarón. The film tells the story of domestic workers in Mexico and is based on Cuarón's own family life and recollections of growing up in a household with a domestic worker. Marcelina gained Cuarón's support for their campaign for domestic workers rights, which considerably raised the profile of their demands. When *Roma* won the Oscar, it also sparked a conversation in the Mexican press on racism, class attitudes to domestic workers, and the normalization of discrimination and injustices in the sector.

Marcelina was one of the founders of the domestic workers' trade union in Mexico (Sindicato Nacional de Trabajadoras del Hogar – SINACTRAHO). SINACTRAHO was instrumental in getting the Mexican government to ratify the C189 and to agree to a pilot Social Security scheme.[6] The trade union has since grown and become more institutional and hierarchical, losing its initial campaigning ethos. Marcelina decided to leave in 2021 to focus on the priorities of her own organization, supporting and empowering domestic workers directly, and she continues to be involved in international campaigns. In March 2022 she launched the Cooperativa para el Desarrollo Integral para las Personas Trabajadoras del Hogar (COODEPTH) to support the development of domestic workers throughout the country.

Ana Laura is also one of the founding members of SINACTRAHO and was involved in a campaign demanding a revision of the Federal Labour Code and ratification of the ILO C189. The union ran an imaginative high-profile campaign using the refrain *Ponte los guantes por los derechos de las trabajadoras del hogar* (Put on your gloves for domestic workers' rights).

They called on members of the public to wear green rubber gloves in support of their campaign and won considerable media coverage. Having achieved important victories through the trade union, Ana Laura, like Marcelina, is also now focussing on working directly with women in the sector:

> 'When a lot of new people joined the union with other ideas, I decided to take a different path. In 2019 I set up an independent group called Domestic Workers Together in Defence of our Rights. I am leading the group, which is a co-operative where we organize and work together informally, comparing experiences and sharing our knowledge. We are building our campaign day by day, but so far it has only been virtual as we haven't been able to meet in person. I am hopeful that when we come out of the pandemic, we will continue strengthening our organization... we are just beginning.' (Ana Laura Aquino, 2022)

From local to global: influencing international policy

The passing of the ILO Convention on Decent Work for Domestic Workers in 2011 led to global recognition that domestic workers have labour rights and has empowered organizations of domestic workers and trade unions to stand up and denounce labour violations. The Convention requires member states to take measures to ensure that domestic workers enjoy protection against all forms of abuse, harassment, and violence and calls for the establishment of mechanisms to protect them and ensure that all complaints are appropriately investigated and prosecuted. It is a tool to support the struggles of organizations of domestic workers advocating with their national governments for labour rights for their sector.

Through global advocacy, the concerns of domestic workers' organizations regarding the implementation of C189 in the region

---

Box 2.2: ILO Convention on Decent Work for Domestic Workers – C189

The ILO C189 recognizes that domestic work continues to be undervalued and invisible, and that it is mainly carried out by women and girls from migrant and disadvantaged communities, who as such are vulnerable to discrimination in employment and other abuses of human rights. There are two Articles in the convention that refer specifically to violence and labour exploitation:

Article 5: 'Each Member shall take measures to ensure that domestic workers enjoy effective protection against all forms of abuse, harassment and violence.'

Article 6: 'Each Member shall take measures to ensure that domestic workers, like workers generally, enjoy fair terms of employment as well as decent working conditions and, if they reside in the household, decent living conditions that respect their privacy.'

The Convention came into force in September 2013 and the ILO has called for all governments to ratify it, but to date only 35 governments have done so (14 of these are in Latin America). Domestic workers' organizations around the world continue the campaign for ratification by their governments and to incorporate these measures within national laws and public policies.

Source: ILO, 2011

---

are being taken on board by the ILO. In Latin America, a virtual regional forum was held in June 2021 to report on the progress and challenges in the implementation in Mexico, Central America, and the Dominican Republic. The forum brought together over 100 domestic workers, ILO officials, leaders from women's organizations, and academics to reflect on steps taken to ensure decent work for domestic workers and the challenges faced in claiming their rights, and an alternative report was prepared on progress in those countries (CARE, 2021). Some of the key findings in the alternative report are that the pandemic has worsened the inequality experienced by domestic workers, and that they do not have effective mechanisms to protect themselves when faced with violations of their labour rights, even when governments have ratified Convention 189. Migrant women domestic workers are especially vulnerable and lack protection, resulting in increased exploitation and higher levels of workplace violence and harassment.

In 2020, CONLACTRAHO joined a new ILO campaign to support the ratification of another international convention protecting all workers from violence and harassment in the workplace. ILO C190 calls on governments and employers to address risk factors in specific sectors and occupations, including actions to protect cleaners and domestic workers who experience unwanted sexual advances, physical assault, and rape by employers (see Box 2.3).

Box 2.3: The ILO Violence and Harassment Convention – ILO C190

The ILO C190 was adopted in 2019 and came into force in June 2021. It is the first international labour instrument that recognizes the right of everyone to work free from violence and harassment. In the preamble to the convention, the ILO recognizes that gender-based violence and harassment (GBVH) in the world of work is an abuse of power, and one of the most prevalent and hidden human rights violations. It affects tens of millions of workers, of all gender identities and across all sectors and occupations, causing physical, psychological, social, and economic harm, undermining economic security and full and equal participation in employment and society.

ILO C190 is inclusive, covering all workers regardless of contractual status, including home-based workers. It does not focus exclusively on women but is especially important to women, including many home-based workers and those in precarious jobs in the informal sector characterized by a high risk of GBVH. According to Recommendation 206, victims of violence and harassment at work should receive compensation for the hurt and illnesses resulting in incapacity to work. It also sets out mechanisms to take forward complaints against employers and for conflict resolution.

Sources: ILO (2019, 2020)

Although 129 countries voted in favour of the C190, to date only 10 governments have committed to ratification. Among them, four are in Latin America. Uruguay was the first country to ratify, and it came into force there in June 2020. Mexico ratified in March 2022 and Argentina and Ecuador will follow later in the year. The next step is to convince other governments to ratify and commit to meet these new international standards in their national laws and policies. Women workers and allies from different sectors and countries are campaigning to secure the adoption of the Convention under the Ratify C190 campaign, bringing organizations together globally to share strategies to encourage governments to ratify the ILO Convention. These include organizations of domestic workers who lobbied to ensure their work experiences were included in the global campaign. As a result of this advocacy, C190 is targeting the root causes of GBVH, including multiple, intersecting forms of discrimination, power relationships, and precarious working arrangements (Conrad, 2021).

CONLACTRAHO is spearheading the Ratify C190 Campaign among its members in Latin America. They produced an illustrated manual for domestic workers that defines harassment and abuse in the workplace and explains what this Convention is about. The manual includes advocacy actions for ratification of the C190 in Latin America and next steps for organizations of domestic workers. They have circulated the manual and a video through social media to all members[7] (CONLACTRAHO, 2020).

Conclusions

Domestic workers' organizations in Latin America have long been fighting for respect and fair treatment: for housework to be valued and recognized as work; for domestic workers' voices to be heard; for domestic workers to be considered as workers with rights and responsibilities, and not as maids or simply 'one of the family'. Domestic workers' struggles are a testament to the resilience of the poorest and most marginalized women, who are standing up and fighting for justice. Domestic workers in Latin America are seeing some results from their activities, for example in the slow shift in social perceptions of domestic workers (as investigated on film), and in the legal situation and status of women who take on cleaning and caring work. There are several factors that have contributed, such as increased access to education, increased awareness of exploitation, and the strengthening of domestic workers' organizations, which by bringing together workers in the sector, has increased their empowerment and self-confidence. Through these organizations, domestic workers have learned about their labour rights and have taken their collective voices and demands into the public arena. Together with their allies they have influenced national policies and the formulation of international legislation, most notably the achievement of the ILO Domestic Workers Convention.

There will always be housework and caring work to be done in households because they are essential for everyone's health and wellbeing. But the power dynamics, which too often result in intersecting forms of violence against women who work in the sector, need further transformation by putting into practice labour laws and international policies that protect the workforce. Importantly, this will come about when cultural perceptions and attitudes toward women and girls who do the cleaning and caring change, and when this work is legitimately valued by society.

Notes

1. The contract, as well as posters listing workers' rights and fair wages, is available to download from the CACEH website www.caceh.org.mx/.
2. The ILO points out that there is a lack of adequate empirical understanding on the situation of Indigenous domestic workers. In 2016 they began a series of country studies to investigate the experiences of Indigenous women entering the domestic work sector. These studies aim to capture numerous aspects related to domestic work, including the reasons that push Indigenous women into domestic work; the circumstances of migration and recruitment; experiences

of working conditions; awareness regarding existing institutions, laws, and policies; and collective efforts, initiatives, or networks by Indigenous women.
3. See Thomson (2021).
4. The International Domestic Workers Network (IDWN) was set up in 2009 following a conference in Amsterdam to promote the mobilization of domestic workers worldwide. IDWN had the support of international organizations such as WIEGO (Women in Informal Employment: Globalizing and Organizing, a global network focused on empowering the working poor, especially women) as well as international trade union federations. The IDWN's Steering Committee accepted 14 domestic workers' organizations' membership applications as the first group of IDWN affiliates, at a meeting held in May 2012. The Founding Congress was held in October 2013, and the IDWN was renamed the International Domestic Workers Federation (IDWF).
5. UTRASD is a solidarity network offering advice and support on employment rights, psycho-social counselling, training on rights, and advocacy to improve legislation.
6. See more at https://www.sinactraho.org.mx.
7. See the video at https://www.youtube.com/watch?v=Git50C FeyRU (CONLACTRAHO, 2021)

Bibliography

Aquino, A.L. (2021), interview with Marilyn Thomson, 1 November, Mexico City (WhatsApp)

Bautista, M. (2022), interview with Marilyn Thomson, 7 April, Mexico City (email correspondence)

CACEH (no date), 'Identidad cultural y no discriminación de las empleadas del hogar', https://caceh.org.mx/quienes-somos

CARE (2018) 'Informe final del estudio de documentación de la violencia y el acoso en el lugar de trabajo contra las trabajadoras remuneradas del hogar en Ecuador, Colombia, México, Honduras y Guatemala', *CARE Regional Programme: Equal Value, Equal Rights & Colectivo de Geografía Crítica del Ecuador*, http://igualva-lorigualesderechos.org/wp-content/uploads/2021/03/ecare-e.pdf

CARE (2021) 'Informe alternativo Convenio 189 OIT: avances y retos en Centroamérica, México y República Dominicana', *CONLACTRAHO Foro regional Junio*, https://igualvalorigualesderechos.org/foro-regional-informe-alternativo-convenio-189-oit-avances-yretos-en-centroamerica-mexico-y-republica-dominicana

CARE & Fundación Bien Humano (2021) 'Actualización del estado de situación de los derechos humanos y laborales de las trabajadoras remuneradas del hogar en Colombia. Estudio C189. *Bien Humano*, https://bienhumano.org/wp-content/uploads/2021/03/Estudio-C189-ISBN-comprimido.pdf

CONLACTRAHO (2020) 'Manual ilustrado del Convenio 190 OIT y su recomendación 206', https://CONLACTRAHO.org/recurso_cat/publicaciones

CONLACTRAHO (2021) 'Demanda por la ratificación del Convenio 190 de la OIT', 23 June, https://www.youtube.com/watch?v=Git50CFeyRU

Conrad, Jenny (2021) 'Ratifying Convention 190 – how countries are encouraging action on workplace violence', *CARE Insights Development Blog*, 25 May, https://insights.careinternational.org.uk/development-blog/ratifying-convention-190-howcountries-are-encouraging-action-on-workplace-violence

Da Silva, N., Granada, L. and Modern, D. (2019) 'The unheard workforce', *LAWRS*, July, pp.8-10, https://lawrs.org.uk/wp-content/uploads/2020/11/Unheard_Workforce_research_2019.pdf

Espinosa Giraldo, A. (2001) *¿Hasta cuándo sin educación? Trabajo doméstico infantil en hogares ajenos en Perú*. Bogotá: Save the Children.

Goldsmith, M. (2013) 'Los espacios internacionales de la participación política de las trabajadoras remuneradas del hogar'. *Revista Estudios Sociales* 45, pp.233-246, http://www.scielo.org.co/scielo.php?script=sci_arttext&pid=S0123-885X2013000100020&lng=en&nrm=iso>. ISSN 0123-885X

IDWFED/FITH (2020) 'Fuertes y unidas enfrentando la pandemia', 12 June, https://idwfed.org/es/recursos/fuertes-y-unidas-enfrentando-la-pandemia-resultados-de-la-encuesta-regional-sobre-el-impacto-del-covid-19-en-las-trabajadoras-del-hogar/@@display-file/attachment_1

ILO (2011) 'C189 – Domestic workers convention, 2011 (no. 189)', https://www.ilo.org/dyn/normlex/en/f?p=NORMLEXPUB:12100:0::NO::P12100_ILO_CODE:C189

ILO (2013) 'Ending child labour in domestic work and protecting young workers from abusive working conditions', https://www.ilo.org/ipec/Informationresources/WCMS_207656/lang--en/index.htm

ILO (2018) 'Report V (1): Ending violence and harassment against women and men in the world of work', https://www.ilo.org/wcmsp5/groups/public/---ed_norm/---relconf/documents/meetingdocument/wcms_553577.pdf

ILO (2019) 'C190 – Violence and harassment convention, 2019 (no. 190)', https://www.ilo.org/dyn/normlex/en/f?p=NORMLEXPUB:12100:0::NO::P12100_ILO_CODE:C190

ILO (2020) 'Policy brief: ILO violence and harassment convention no. 190 and recommendation no. 206', https://www.ilo.org/wcmsp5/groups/public/---ed_dialogue/---actrav/documents/briefingnote/wcms_749786.pdf

ILO (2022) 'COVID-19: guidance for occupational safety and health for employers and domestic workers', https://www.ilo.org/global/

topics/safety-and-health-at-work/news/WCMS_834920/lang--en/
index

Mlambo-Ngcuka, P. (2020) 'Violence against women and girls: the shadow pandemic', 6 April, https://www.unwomen.org/en/news/stories/2020/4/statement-ed-phumzile-violence-against-women-during-pandemic

Moynihan K. (2020) 'Filmography', in: Osborne E. and Ruiz-Alfaro S. (eds.) *Domestic labor in twenty-first century Latin American cinema.* London: Palgrave Macmillan, https://doi.org/10.1007/978-3-030-33296-9_11

Thomson, M (2021) 'Organisations | Latin American Women's Rights Service (LAWRS)', *Latin America Bureau*, 15 October, https://lab.org.uk/wrv-organisations-lawrs

UN Women/ILO/CLAC (2020) 'Domestic workers in Latin America and the Caribbean during the Covid-19 crisis', Brief V.1.1.12.06.2020, https://www.ilo.org/wcmsp5/groups/public/---americas/---ro-lima/documents/publication/wcms_751773.pdf

UN Women (2020) 'Intersectional feminism: what it means and why it matters', https://www.unwomen.org/en/news/stories/2020/6/explainer-intersectional-feminism-what-it-means-and-why-it-matters

CHAPTER 3
'It is a very tough fight': Abortion as a battleground over women's rights in Latin America

Jelke Boesten and Andrea Espinoza

Throughout the Americas, there are tensions and contradictions around the fulfilment and protection of reproductive rights. Several major feminist wins have been aggressively resisted and even reversed by conservative forces. So, what are these battles about? Do they concern abortion, the 'right to life', women's rights, or still something more complex? How can we understand the energy invested by activists on both sides of the spectrum, their gains and losses? And what does this ultimately mean for women's rights and gender equality in Latin America and beyond?

The battle over legal abortion is important for its own sake; however, the stakes are much higher. The issue broaches bodily and sexual autonomy, including against violence. It concerns women's right to control their own lives without the imposition of a harmful patriarchal order, and the equal access to services. Abortion is the main field allowing conservative forces to mobilize religious, 'pro-life', hetero-normative morality – in support of a range of oppressive gender structures and norms far beyond abortion. Therefore, activism for legal abortion is central to a broader movement for inclusive citizenship, women's equal rights, a life free from violence, and sexual and gender diversity.

Abortion politics and reproductive health in general is a site of multiple intersecting violences: the lack of healthcare services is infrastructural violence (McIlwaine, see Chapter 5); the neglect of poor, Black and Indigenous women in particular is a form of structural violence; the moral discourses surrounding women's fertility impose norms about subordinate gender roles and are forms of normative violence; and of course, ultimately, many of these forms of so-called 'indirect violence' are grounded in, and form legitimate discourses of, sexual and physical violence against women, girls, and LGBTQ+ communities. Reproductive health is at the core of women's bodily autonomy and freedom and hence, central to the feminist fight for women's rights and gender equality. In this chapter we will examine the successes of the feminist movement in fighting this battle over the last 10 or so years and we will contrast this with the increasingly fierce and broad-based conservative backlash against emancipatory progress.

Activism

Argentina's political win in December 2020 over the legalization of elective abortion was the result of years of activism and lobbying by feminist activists and their allies. Prior to this, Argentina had a restrictive law in place which allowed abortion only when the pregnancy threatened the woman's health, or in cases of rape. This legal framework was part of the Argentine Penal Code from 1921. In 2012, the law was expanded with the decriminalization of abortion for all victims of sexual abuse, but implementation was limited. Then finally, in December 2020, the pro-choice movement won over the senate with a bill that allows for free and legal abortion for all in pregnancies up to 14 weeks. In the same session, the senate adopted a bill to provide better pre-and post-natal healthcare.

This widely celebrated victory was the result of intense campaigning, in recent years symbolized by the green *pañuelos*, or kerchiefs, worn by pro-choice activists as bandanas, scarfs, bracelets, tops, and face coverings. But Argentina has a long history of grassroots activism for the legalization of abortion. In the early 1980s, abortion was very much

Figure 3.1: Argentine feminist Verónica Gago argues that the power of feminist mobilization is potentially 'changing everything'. Credit: Verso Books

part of feminist campaigns for sexual liberation: one iconic image from the early Argentinian feminist agenda in 1983 shows feminist activist María Elena Oddone with a banner reading, 'No to maternity, yes to pleasure'.

The campaign later transitioned from a focus on liberation to a rights-based approach. In March 1988, a group of women created the Right to Abortion Commission, an organization pioneering the fight to discuss abortion as a right. During the 1990s the pro-choice agenda grew and extended across Argentina. In November 1990, feminist groups conducted the Fifth Feminist Latin America-Caribbean Meeting in San Bernardo, Argentina, and the Right to Abortion Commission coordinated the first workshops called 'Abortion as a Right'. Two years later, in 1992, this commission presented the first legal reform bill to parliament. It did not get voted through.

In the 2000s, the pro-choice campaign again adapted, this time to include a more health-based approach. In 2005, the campaign highlighted the safety of abortions, with multiple organizations aligning in the National Campaign for the Right to Legal, Safe and Free Abortion. The campaign developed the pro-choice movement as a whole, presenting projects to decriminalize abortion in 2007, 2010, 2012, 2014, and, accompanied by street protests, in 2018. The 2018 project was discussed in and approved by parliament but was rejected by the Senate. Nevertheless, massive pro-abortion mobilizations took place in 2019 and 2020 as well, keeping the demands squarely on the public agenda. In fact, President Alberto Fernández made legal, safe, and free abortion part of his electoral campaign in 2019, highlighting the toll that clandestine terminations claim on women and thus on wider society and the healthcare system. As a sign of the changing times, he was elected, and he followed through in presenting the successful pro-abortion bill to parliament and senate. The win created impetus throughout Latin America to continue the fight for women's rights, despite powerful and aggressive transnational conservative forces actively undermining gender equality and women's citizenship. Mexican pro-choice activists adopted the green *pañuelo* for their campaigns and, following Argentina, in September 2021 Mexico effectively decriminalized abortion – despite the reverse action in its neighbouring state, Texas, which in the same month *criminalized* all abortion after six weeks of gestation.

As in other parts of Latin America, abortion was not only illegal but actively prosecuted and penalized in Mexico through the criminal courts. After years of activism, in September 2021 the Supreme Court ruled that penalizing women for terminating a pregnancy is unconstitutional and against women's right to decide over their own lives - effectively decriminalizing abortion following a logic of human rights. This set a precedent to further amplify the provision of abortion, making it 'legal, free, and safe'. On 21 February 2022, the Colombian Constitutional Court decriminalized abortion up to 24 weeks of gestation, allowing abortion on demand. But Ana Cristina González, a Colombian activist for Movimiento Causa Justa, explains that the ruling of the Constitutional Court does not mean that the fight is over:

> 'We need to move the conversation about abortion away from the criminal field, because even with the new legal framework, abortion is still seen as a crime, even if in a symbolic way. In that sense, it continues to deprive women of the opportunity to be full citizens whose autonomy and freedom are respected and valued'. (El Tiempo, 2022)

These Argentinian, Mexican, and Colombian wins are important for women's rights and gender equality throughout the region, even if actual access to abortion remains a complex issue often highly influenced by local medical personnel and pressure groups. In Ecuador, for example, on 17 February 2022, the National Assembly discussed a law to allow abortion in cases of rape up to 22 weeks of gestation. However, for the law to pass, the lawmakers reduced the time to 12 weeks and 18 weeks in exceptional cases. Ana Vera, director of Surkuna, an Ecuadorian feminist organization, says:

> 'Ecuador has not accomplished an abortion law that will ensure girls, women, and pregnant people access to this service... For that reason, we must go back to the Constitutional Court for the obstacles to be erased. But it's going to be a very tough fight'. (Radio Pichincha, 2022)

In the words of Argentinian scholar and activist Marianna Romero, who recently spoke on *BBC Woman's Hour* (2022), the victory in Colombia is 'huge, a milestone for women in Latin America'. However, activists find that there is still much to be done, as access to services is often only realistic for those with higher education and wealth: i.e. for whiter middle and upper classes, not for the poor and largely Black, Indigenous, or mestiza (mixed) population.

The landscape of abortion rights

The countries in Latin America and the Caribbean where abortion is legal are Cuba (since 1965), Guyana (since 1995), Puerto Rico (since 1937), Uruguay (since 2012), Argentina (since December 2020), Mexico (since September 2021), and Colombia (since February 2022). In other countries like the Dominican Republic, El Salvador, Haiti, Honduras, Nicaragua, and Suriname, abortion is prohibited altogether with no explicit legal exception. In most Latin American countries, the legal framework presents at least one exception - that is, when a pregnant woman's life is at risk. There are other conditions with which to access legal abortion in the region, but they vary according to country. For example, in Brazil, since 2012, abortion is an option when the foetus has anencephaly, a congenital brain malformation. Before the Colombian Constitutional Court decriminalized abortion, in 2011 the Court issued a clarification establishing that the risk to the woman's mental health was reason enough to carry out a voluntary interruption of pregnancy. Nonetheless, the existence of these basic legal exceptions did not mean that the service became accessible because of restrictions related to access to medicine, infrastructure, or professionals to execute the process (conscientious objection). Similarly, the clarification did not ensure that women would not be persecuted or harassed when trying to access the service, especially using the public health system.

The extent of women's vulnerability is proportional to other factors like poverty and ethnicity. In the case of Mexico, according to a report produced by the feminist organization Grupo de Información de Reproducción Elegida (GIRE), women living in poverty and Indigenous women are nine times more likely to have an unsafe abortion than women with greater economic possibilities, more education, and who do not belong to Indigenous groups (GIRE, 2015). The same is true for other countries: your socio-economic status largely determines your access to reproductive healthcare, including abortion.

Some countries include rape and incest as valid reasons to allow an abortion, but this is often contested. Brazil, Colombia, and Chile decriminalized abortions in cases of rape, but in other countries like Peru, Venezuela, Paraguay, and Guatemala, it is still prohibited and punished with prison sentences ranging from months to several years. In Ecuador until April 2021, abortions in cases of rape were only permitted for women with a mental disability. In April, the Constitutional Court ruled that abortion should be decriminalized in all cases of rape. However, even in cases where abortion due to rape is decriminalized, access is not secured and harassment in the public health system is a real possibility.

The lack of access in cases of rape has gained particular attention as it has become clear how many underage girls are forced to continue with pregnancies after rape. Such structural violence - how the lack of service provision physically and mentally harms people, particularly the non-privileged - is both an example of infrastructural violence

(McIlwaine, see Chapter 5), as well as normative violence (Butler 2004, Boesten 2011). While the lack of service is partly the consequence of a lack of a functioning healthcare infrastructure, it is likewise the moral judgement of healthcare personnel to deny children a legal abortion. In this refusal, the initial crime of rape is wilfully ignored. The blame is squarely put on the victims, unnecessarily forcing them to carry the assault and accompanying shame and guilt with them – in many cases for the rest of their lives.

There is little doubt that a majority of child and teenage pregnancies are the result of rape: an older study (1996) in a maternity ward of the biggest public hospital in Lima indicated that 90 per cent of girls under the age of 18 giving birth had conceived following rape. Information from CLADEM-Peru (Comité de América Latina y el Caribe para la Defensa de los Derechos de las Mujeres, a feminist network utilizing the rule of law to uphold women's rights in Latin America and the Caribbean) shows that forced motherhood after rape in children is increasing. In Peru there was a 31 per cent increase in the number of babies born to 11 to 14-year-olds from 2016 to 2018 (CLADEM, 2021). As the age of consent in Peru is 14, all these cases are statutorily the result of rape. Pregnancies in children even younger than 11 have sparked outrage: in the pandemic year 2020, Peru saw a tripling of child mothers, from 9 in 2019 to 26 in 2020. Considering this was in a time in which families were forced to live behind closed doors during a national lockdown, there is no doubt that these children were abused by those supposed to care for them. Such cases have given new impetus in the pro-abortion camp with slogans such as #NiñasNoMadres. This campaign not only supports abortion in cases of underage girls, but also highlights the need for debate on how society – and the judiciary – deals with rape and incest.

While clearly there is still much to do before all women and girls have free autonomy over their bodies, sexuality, and fertility; recent developments are changing the debate. For example, instead of using the term '*aborto*', there is a growing trend to discuss 'legal inter-ruption of pregnancy' and 'voluntary interruption of pregnancy'. This distinction makes a difference as it moves from the highly stigmatized term 'abortion' to a wording based on access to rights and focusing on women's control over their bodies. Through this fight, feminist organi-zations have demonstrated the strength and transformative power of grassroots organization. While the most well-known example is the work in Argentina by the collectives organized through the National Campaign for the Rights to Legal, Safe and Free Abortion; in Ecuador the Constitutional Court ruling was a success because of demands presented by feminist collectives like Challenge Foundation, the

National Coalition of Women, and the Front for the Defence of Sexual Rights and Dignity. In Colombia, several women's organizations came together under the Just Cause Movement to lobby for the legalization of abortion, successful in February 2022. Peruvian feminists are mobilizing to draw on these examples and push for change in their own country. Scholar-activist Angélica Motta states on Facebook:

> 'We need to study the experiences of other Latin American countries that managed to legalize abortion. We have a tough fight ahead of us, but we can learn from our *compañeras.*' (Motta, 2022)

Box 3.1: The fight for reproductive rights in El Salvador

Marilyn Thomson

El Salvador not only has one of the most restrictive abortion laws in the world, but also systematically persecutes women and girls under this law, even when they experience miscarriages, stillbirths, or obstetric complications. Dozens of women are jailed for the deaths of their foetuses in cases where they had suffered miscarriages or stillbirths. According to Center for Reproductive Rights, a global legal advocacy organization, an estimated 5,000 abortions occur illegally in El Salvador every year. Women who are found to have had an abortion face between two and eight years' imprisonment, which can rise to 40 years if they are found guilty of aggravated homicide.

Previous access to therapeutic and emergency abortion was repealed in 1997 and now the law bans abortion in all circumstances, including abortions to a woman's life. In 1999, a constitutional amendment was passed declaring that life begins at conception, and prosecutors use this to convert charges against women suspected of having an abortion to aggravated homicide. The Penal Code has strict criminal penalties for anyone who procures an abortion or allows one to be procured. Health professionals are obliged to report a suspected abortion to the police and face harsh criminal sanctions for performing emergency abortions or medical treatment that unintentionally results in a miscarriage. To do so risks up to 12 years' imprisonment and the removal of their licence to practice medicine.

As a result of this law, women and girls in El Salvador are not only criminalized for obstetric complications during pregnancy but are denied access to medical care to preserve their life or their physical and mental health, and are unable to receive treatment, even when an emergency termination of their pregnancy is required to save their lives. This includes ectopic pregnancies, which cannot legally be treated in El Salvador until the foetal heartbeat stops or the fallopian tube ruptures. Medical staff members are forced to leave women to enter a medical emergency rather than giving them timely medical care.

In 2014, a feminist group called The Citizens' Coalition for the Decriminalization of Abortion (ACDATEE) began a campaign to highlight the cases of 129 women who were imprisoned for abortion and 26 other women who were prosecuted for aggravated homicide after an abortion, miscarriage, or stillbirth. The Las 17 campaign called for the freedom and pardon of 17 of the women who had been wrongly sentenced to life imprisonment charged with murder, because their trials had been flawed and did not meet international standards, and their convictions were made in the absence of any direct evidence.

ACDATEE also works to influence public opinion and broaden the debate on abortion through media work and engaging with networks of women's groups. They work with medical professionals and organizations to develop a protocol on patient confidentiality and professional ethics in relation to reproductive healthcare. ACDATEE also provides legal counsel and representation for women prosecuted under these laws and aims to secure their release.

Alongside Amnesty International and various other organizations, ACTADEE ran a global campaign to gather support for a petition demanding the women be released from prison. In August 2017, they presented almost 90,000 supporting signatures to the Salvadorean parliament. This international campaign helped the decriminalization movement to gain ground in El Salvador but it provoked backlash from religious fundamentalists and right-wing conservative groups, including a negative media campaign against multiple women's organizations who called for decriminalization. In his election 2019 campaign, Nayib Bukele promised to reform the law, but since being elected president he has failed to enact these promises. His government has become increasingly authoritarian and in November 2021, prosecutors raided the offices of seven charities and groups working on education, human rights, health, and women's rights and proposed a bill that requires civil society organizations who receive overseas funding to register as 'foreign agents' – in an effort to control social movements.

In November 2021, the Inter-American Court of Human Rights heard the case of Manuela, one of the women who died in prison from cancer after receiving inadequate medical diagnosis and treatment. Manuela had been serving a 30-year prison sentence for aggravated homicide after a miscarriage. Her family brought her case against the government, with support from ACTADEE and the Center for Reproductive Rights. In a landmark ruling, the Court found the State of El Salvador responsible for Manuela's death and declared they must pay reparations to Manuela's family, adopt structural measures towards decriminalizing abortion, develop comprehensive sexual education policies, and guarantee doctor-patient confidentiality. 'The Inter-American court has done justice by recognising Manuela was another victim of an unjust legal context that originates in the absolute prohibition of abortion,' stated Morena Herrera, ACTADEE (Daniels, 2021).

Sources: CAWN (2015), Centre for Reproductive Rights (2012), Daniels (2021)

Counter-movement

Progressive developments are often met with increasingly vocal and visible resistance from conservative forces throughout Latin America. This moral conservatism largely aligns with right-wing political movements, although that is not the case everywhere: Peru just elected former schoolteacher and union leader Pedro Castillo to the presidency. Castillo is both on the far left and on the morally conservative side of politics; against abortion, sex education, and LGBTQ+ rights. Nicaragua's president Daniel Ortega was once leftist and progressive but is now a dictator steeped in extreme moral conservativism, with one of the most brutal anti-abortion penal systems in the region.

Nevertheless, these are political outliers. Generally, the wave of conservative anti-abortion activism has emerged under the wings of a post-Pink Tide move to the right. While conservative right-wing movements have been associated with economic interests and hence, economic elites; in recent years, conservative morality politics has drawn in more grassroots, often religious, movements that protest against abortion, sexual diversity, and sex education in schools. What these movements have in common, as Lindsay Mayka and Amy Erica Smith argue (2021), is a belief in a rigid binary gender order and natural societal hierarchies. In this light, the anti-abortion lobby clearly focuses on controlling women, their labour, and their sexuality. For some, anti-abortion sentiment might be about ideas around the start of life - at conception or somewhere along the way of gestation - but its politics are clearly aimed at maintaining the patriarchy.

Pro-life, against women

The idea that pro-life politics is about respect for life is immediately undercut by the harm it does to the lives of women and children. According to the authoritative Alan Guttmacher Institute (2018), as of 2017, more than 24 million women of reproductive age in Latin America and the Caribbean have an unmet need for modern contraception - and get pregnant when they do not want to. As of 2010-2014, Latin America and the Caribbean had the highest rate of unintended pregnancy of any world region - 96 per 1,000 women aged 15-44. In the subregion of the Caribbean, the rate was 116 unintended pregnancies per 1,000 women. An estimated 14 million unintended pregnancies occur each year in Latin America and the Caribbean: of these, nearly half (46 per cent) end in abortion. A considerable proportion of these will be executed under clandestine circumstances, at home or in unprofessional and unaccountable 'clinics'. And yearly, about 760,000 women are treated for complications due to unsafe abortions, and about 900 women die.

A particular point to highlight here is the use of the category 'unintended pregnancy', especially when the pregnant woman is a minor - as we saw above in the case of forced motherhood among children. 'Unintended pregnancy' blurs the line between health concerns and the recognition of possible criminal behaviour (sexual violence) against women and girls. For example, in Bolivia, according to data from the Ministry of Health through the National Health Information Service (SNIS), from January to July 2020, 19,233 cases of pregnancies in girls and adolescents were registered - that is 90 pregnancies per day. In the case of pregnancy in girls under 15 years of age, the figure (953) amounts to four pregnancies per day. The authorities pointed out that most cases of pregnancies in children under 15 years of age result from sexual violence carried out by aggressors who are part of the family environment or close to the victim. It is particularly relevant to point out that this number of child and teenage pregnancies is registered in the health system and not the legal system, falling into a category of unintended pregnancy or unintended pregnancy of a minor, and not as sexual abuse, a criminal act. Abortion is often still not an option for these girls. In El Salvador (see above), children under 14 who abort are imprisoned, even if the age of consent is 18, and hence, all such cases are statutory cases of rape.

Girls having to give birth after rape is forced motherhood; it truncates their dreams and forces them to live with the trauma, stigma, and blame of having been raped. As these cases are treated in the media, in public policy, and in medical settings as unintended pregnancies rather than violence, rapists are never held responsible. In fact, pro-life activists and politicians omit men from their consider-ations – as fathers and as rapists. This again confirms that a 'pro-life' stance is a cruel misogynist politics aimed at disciplining women.

So, what do conservative forces gain from such a harmful patriarchal politics? Rigid female gender roles and a focus among women and girls on reproducing life provides care for children, men, the chronically ill, and elderly. They are effectively free labour to a society in which the state fails to provide social care and instead focuses on a male labour market seeking the accumulation of capital. Returning to a restrictive sexual morality fits a neoliberal order that is increasingly undermined by growing gender equality, increased sexual diversity, and the emancipation and ascent of racialized minorities.

Pro-abortion, pro-inclusion

Abortion is an intersectional issue: poor, rural, and Indigenous women have least access to safe abortion, and least access to sex education and other forms of birth control. Institutional discrimi-nation based on gender, race, and class further prevents poorer women of Indigenous, mixed, and Afro descent from adequately accessing reproductive health services. In addition, the fact that the pro-life movement promotes heteronormative sexual behaviours further hinders the possibility of sexual diversity, undermining the lives of LGBTQ+ individuals.

The struggle for abortion rights is therefore part of an inclusive struggle for reproductive and sexual rights - including sex education for all, free and good reproductive healthcare, and access to birth control and maternity care. While abortion is the battleground, access to a range of improved services has been on the agenda for women's movements since the early 1980s. Most middle-class urban women have access to reproductive healthcare and modern birth control methods, but rural women, poor women, and otherwise marginalized groups have not.

Box 3.2: Somos 2074 y Muchas Más

Between 1996 and 1998, the government of Alberto Fujimori in Peru decided to circumvent battles with conservative forces over access to education, information, and decent public reproductive health services by establishing a forceful National Programme for Family Planning and Reproductive Health. The programme aimed to bring family planning – including the controversial voluntary sterilization procedure – to neglected, poor, and rural regions. USAID provided funding, and feminist NGO Manuela Ramos was supposed to provide awareness and information at community level. By 1998 it became clear that the programme was, in fact, an aggressive campaign based on a quota system that aimed to sterilize as many women as possible to rapidly reduce the birth rate among poor Indigenous people.

About 300,000 women and some men were sterilized in this period. Not all were forced, but few had adequate information that would have enabled them to provide informed consent. The programme used mobile campaigns and small rural healthcare centres with poor hygiene standards and few medical supplies. Women were lured with food donations. Others were sterilized just after giving birth. And some – at least 2074 – were physically forced to undergo the procedure. At least one woman died.

According to feminist, scholar, and congresswoman Rocío Silva Santisteban (2020), the sterilizations represented 'a form of sexual violence and a form of biopolitical control over the bodies of brown women, Indigenous, mestiza, and poor women who had no means to raise their voices and who had no idea what their rights were' (DW, 2021).

Somos 2074 y Muchas Más is an association of feminist organizations and networks that campaigns for justice for the victims of what is generally known as 'forced sterilizations'. The group organizes public campaigns on social media and on the streets, works with rural women's organizations to support their claims, and provides a platform for activism. Different governments have washed their hands of the issue and refused a proper investigation into the matter but in October 2021, the case was accepted for criminal investigation by the National Criminal Court. Rocío Silva Santisteban observes that this will be a 'mega trial, the first in Peru of this kind of international importance, because almost 1,700 victims are involved, and they all demand public defence from the Peruvian State.'

Sources: Boesten (2010), DEMUS (n/d), DW (2021)

Sex education

Access to information is paramount for the management of fertility, as is access to types of sex education that might reduce gendered stereotypes about sex and sexuality. But sex education has also been

Figure 3.2: Woman from the campaign Somos 2074 y Muchas Más demonstrates against impunity. Credit: Somos 2074 y Muchas Más

a battleground: many countries throughout Latin America have well-designed, progressive, and inclusive sex education guidelines prepared by knowledgeable policymakers and embedded in internationally agreed guidelines. However, in several countries, a new wave of moral conservatives have successfully opposed these programmes.

From 2011, Ecuador started to implement the National Strategy for Family Planning and to Prevent Adolescent Pregnancy (ENIPLA). The programme defined gender as a social construct that goes beyond the biological classification of women and men. It targeted adolescents and engaged with them through high school meetings, information brochures, social media, and radio programs. The policy briefs explained that ENIPLA referred to sexuality as a natural and significant part of how people experience their lives. The programme also offered information about masturbation, biological changes, sexual curiosity, and contraception through a national public campaign. The programme recognized and addressed sex, sexual identity, gender roles, eroticism, pleasure, and intimacy. However, in 2015, the (leftist) president Rafael Correa replaced the programme with a conservative family-focused programme.

In Peru, comprehensive sex and gender education has been a field of contention since the mid-1990s. Progressive policymakers and education specialists have designed and delivered guidelines for schools multiple times but have always been obstructed by influential religious lobbyists close to the government. In 2016, the Peruvian government finally adopted a sex and gender education school curriculum for all. However, conservative Evangelical civil society organizations with links to politicians in the senate organized protests in the movement #ConMisHijosNoTeMetas (Leave My Kids Alone), opposing gender equality and sexual diversity. They accused the government of promoting 'sexual perversion and identity confusion' and even forced the education minister out. In 2019, the Supreme Court ruled against the objections and thereby confirmed that a gender perspective in the national curriculum was desirable (Rousseau, 2020). Implementation is, of course, a major issue until all teachers are well-trained to deliver such a programme.

The role of feminists

The Argentine feminist activist and scholar Verónica Gago, following activists throughout Latin America, observes that there is an essential link between struggles over land, the environment, and women's bodies (2020). She holds that the neoliberal heteropatriarchal order dominates the land and people for the financial gain of the few. Gago speaks of the body-territory, noting how women's bodies are often in the middle of struggles over land (see Chapter 4). She holds that literally and figuratively, women are treated as territory, as property of others, as bodies that can be owned and invaded. This analysis is not only a condemnation of the neoliberal heteropatriarchal order and its conservative cheerleaders, but it has also created a powerful under-standing of feminist activism as full of social and political potential, or, in Gago's words, '*potencia feminista*' - feminist power.

During the mass pro-abortion mobilizations between 2018 and 2020 in Argentina, feminist organizations banded together through a democratic practice of assembly, uniting women from all walks of life in solidarity through a women's strike. Removing women's labour in the workplace, in homes, and in community organizations is an economic strategy that highlights the value of women's labour beyond the salaried labour market. It also generates a notion of the embodied and territorial experience that is women's labour, women's activism, and women's rights. The strike, based on the idea of economic value, is a protest against the use and abuse of women's and feminized bodies; a campaign for the right for women, trans people, and transvestites to a life free from violence; and a campaign for abortion, equal pay, equal opportunities, and welfare.

Gago explains how throughout this process, differences among women were overcome through a practice of listening. For example, thanks to collective debate between different groups of activists, it became clear that women working in community food banks and soup kitchens were unwilling to stop supplying food during the strike; they did not want to leave the poor without their daily meal. Together the women found a compromise: they would coordinate daily food deliveries and provide access to the kitchens, but they would not actually prepare the food themselves that day, leaving the task to other community members. As such, the feminist movement in Argentina found a powerful way to mobilize vast numbers of women and their allies, occupy political and actual space (territory), contribute to social change, and provide valuable intellectual ideas. The power of feminist mobilization is potentially 'changing everything', Gago argues.

Box 3.3: Interview with Verónica Gago, Argentinian activist of NiUnaMenos and author of *Feminist International, or How to Change Everything* (2020)

On the body-territory: 'The term 'body-territory' allows us to see the personal dimension of power struggles, but also how we are connected with wider territories and that is also useful so that we think beyond our individual stories and experiences. It allows us to make connections between the personal and the political, and the political and material dimensions of this body we have. In Latin America our struggles are strongly related to extractivist exploitation – of land and bodies – which the body-territory makes visible.'

On the feminist strike: 'The feminist strike becomes more powerful every year, confronting the crisis with a deeper and more transnational movement. The feminist strike can include different kinds of labour issues and struggles. New forms of exploitation are getting more and more aggressive, and more and more cruel against certain bodies and certain territories, and these are political questions put to the table by the feminist strike.'

On transnational feminism: 'The transnational dimension of the present moment involves the nurturing of activism across borders: activists translate slogans and graffitis, they borrow symbols [eg. the green pañuelo to symbolize pro-abortion rights], and we work together to support each other.'

'In Peru, NiUnaMenos was a mass mobilization that has been translated into different objectives, from campaigns against feminicide to the preparation and inclusion of feminist agendas and feminist leaders in electoral politics. It has been a point of departure for a broad-based movement. This shows that one good slogan, NiUnaMenos, can become a political movement, provide a diagnosis of machista violence, and help turn victimhood into political action. While each country has its own trajectory and process, we share similar objectives and learn from each other.'

'It is important to note that feminist mobilization and conceptual knowledge is moving from the South to the North. The public performance of Las Tesis, translated and performed around the world, has contributed to mobilization globally, but I am also talking about how migrant workers in the North organize against violence, or for better labour conditions in domestic work.'

On 'How to Change Everything': 'Feminism is no longer an ˌexclusive language; we are experiencing a practical democratization of feminism. We are in a transversal debate about how we should organize everything: from food to health to knowledge, sexual and affective relations, as well as labour, housing, and finance. We are organizing to politicize each aspect of everyday life. And this is amazing. We have the experience and knowledge as a movement, so I think we can do this, change everything.'

Source: Boesten and Martin (2021)

Conclusion

The right to abortion is perhaps the most salient contemporary battle-ground for women's rights and gender equality. Alliances between right-wing political and economic elites and conservative-religious groups from other socioeconomic classes have created powerful counter-movements against abortion, reproductive rights, sexual diversity, and gender equality more broadly. Arguments about the 'right to life' of foetuses are set against arguments for women's bodily autonomy, and in large parts of Latin America, these 'pro-life' arguments even subordinate arguments around criminal acts: underage girls raped and impregnated are forced to carry babies to term without recourse to justice. The intersectional vulnerabilities of poor, Black, Indigenous, and mestiza women and minors make it even more important to legalize abortion and work towards universal accessibility.

This concerning landscape is brightened by the fierce resistance of the many local and regional mobiliszations for abortion rights, and the alliances between progressive forces. Argentina and Mexico recently fully legalized abortion; the result of sustained mobilization across different sectors and providing new fields for debate throughout the region. As we enter a new political era, with a feminism that is much more vocal, visible and with more political power – the new feminist government in Chile, installed in early 2022, is certainly the example we will all be looking at – and a global conservative right-wing movement that may be losing its grip, we must look at the future with hope and strength and the will to change everything. 'It is a very tough fight', but it is not at all lost.

Bibliography

BBC Woman's Hour, 'Lucy Cooke on the female of the species, furniture poverty, threads', *BBC Radio 4*, 1 March, https://www.bbc.co.uk/programmes/m0014wt2

Boesten, J.J. (2010) *Intersecting inequalities: women and social policy in Peru.* University Park, Pennsylvania: Penn State University Press

Boesten, J. and Martin, P. (2021) 'Veronica Gago on feminist power', *WORLD: we got this* [podcast], 21 February, https://lab.org.uk/wrv-veronica-gago-on-feminist-power

Centre for Reproductive Rights (2012) 'Manuela v. El Salvador (Inter-American Court of Human Rights)', 21 March, https://reproductiverights.org/case/manuela-v-el-salvadorinter-american-court-of-human-rights

CLADEM-Peru (2021) 'Informe nacional sobre embarazo infantil forzado en el Perú: avances en su atención y desafíos (2018-2021)', https://cladem.org/principales-acciones-peru/informe-nacional-sobre-embarazo-infantil-forzado-en-el-peru-suatencion-y-desafios-2018-2021

Daniels, J.P. (2021) 'El Salvador 'responsible for death of woman jailed after miscarriage', *The Guardian*, 2 December, https://www.theguardian.com/global-development/2021/dec/02/el-salvador-responsible-for-death-of-woman-jailed-after-miscarriage

DEMUS (no date) 'Somos 2074 y muchas más', https://www.demus.org.pe/campanas/somos-2074-y-muchas-mas

DW (2021) 'Perú y la herida de las esterilizaciones forzadas: una "deuda histórica"', *DW*, 14 February, https://www.elmostrador.cl/braga/2021/02/14/peru-y-la-herida-de-las-esterilizaciones-forzadasuna-deuda-historica

Gago, V. (2020) *Feminist international: how to change everything.* London: Verso Books.

Grupo de Información de Reproducción Elegida (2015) 'Niñas y mujeres sin justicia', *GIRE* https://gire.org.mx/publicaciones/ninas-y-mujeres-sin-justicia-derechos-reproductivos-en-mexico

Mayka, L. and Smith, A.E. (2021), 'Introduction the grassroots right in Latin America: patterns, causes, and consequences', *Latin American Politics and Society* 63(1), pp.1–20.

Motta, A. (2022) Angélica Motta [Facebook post] 17 March, https://l.facebook.com/l.php?u=https%3A%2F%2Ffeminista.com%2Fana-cristina-gonzalez-aborto-colombia%2F&h=AT2GCKtjysEbhWuUFpcewIEoV_3Q6BwYTzM3MOiXvwWuJPtgZsoYJ15msSZ_7cQyJ4MMRQ5Hn89tt2BtjT-dUiHpdsdJ7SDHvKMpbXk-ZuitjZeyYPpahWT5xQc0UqKg_CyWZ3i4&s=1

Radio Pichincha (2022), 'Punto noticias 1ra emisión', 22 February, https://www.youtube.com/watch?v=D3PztRpgG8c&ab_channel=RadioPichincha

Rousseau, S. (2020) 'Antigender activism in Peru and its impact on state policy', *Politics & Gender* 16(1)

Tendencias El Tiempo (2022) 'Despenalización del aborto: así reaccionan políticos a decisión de la Corte', *El Tiempo*, 22 February, https://www.eltiempo.com/justicia/cortes/despenalizacion-del-aborto-en-colombia-reacciones-a-la-decision-653263

CHAPTER 4

'Violence on our lands, violence on our bodies': Women resisting land grabbing and environmental violence

Patricia Muñoz Cabrera

Land grabbing is the harmful acquisition of large swaths of land, often taken by private investors and agribusinesses to be leased long term for agricultural activity. Contentiously, these sellers often operate in the legal 'grey areas' between traditional land rights and modern property laws (Global Agriculture, no date), making it difficult for inhabitants of these lands, especially Indigenous and Afro descendant communities, to claim their rights. Since the year 2000, land grabbing has become a key element of development agendas in Latin America, promoted by governments and international financial institutions through so-called 'land markets' as a strategy to attract foreign direct investment in order to boost economic growth. This has contributed to widespread violence and dispossession. As a woman leader from ANAMURI, the National Association of Rural and Indigenous Women in Chile, states:

> 'Our bodies continue to be the site of patriarchal domination, economic domination, economic wars for land grabbing, and wars to privatize our rivers, lands, and territories. We struggle for the structural transformation of the patriarchal and capitalist systems.' (ANAMURI, 2017)

This chapter discusses the impacts of land grabbing on rural, peasant, Indigenous, and Afro-descendant women living in areas rich in natural resources. It highlights the negative impacts of land grabbing on women's fundamental human rights, their bodies, and their territories, and details some of their struggles to counter this harm. The chapter also discusses women's proposals to policymakers to implement economic models enshrined in fundamental human rights, in particular women's rights, including the right to a life free from land grabbing-related violence. Finally, the chapter maps out women's relentless work to raise awareness, influence policymakers, and mobilize constituencies on women's human rights and nature's rights at the local, national, and international levels.

Land grabbing as a harmful practice

'Land grabbing is doing harm to our bodies, our lands, our territories, and their ecosystems.' (Ercilia Araya, 2022).

A large majority of rural, peasant, Indigenous, and Afro-descendant communities are enduring the impacts of large-scale agribusiness and resource extraction (mining), which has resulted in the denial of land rights, the loss of traditional livelihoods, widespread territorial dispossession, and environmental contamination.

Across the region, land grabbing for monoculture (to establish single-crop plantations of sugarcane, oil palm, eucalyptus, and soybeans) has led to the forced displacement of entire communities. In Guatemala, Maya Q'eqchi' Indigenous people, many of whom fled their region during the country's 36-year civil war, have endured land dispossession, increased poverty, hunger, and overall unemployment.

Cláudia from the Tupinikim and Guaraní Indigenous Women's Commission, Pau-Brasil, explains the devastating effects of land grabbed for monoculture on her community and ecosystem:

'Because of the plantations... the soil is sandy. That's because of the eucalyptus trees, because they took all of the vitamins out of the soil... before the rivers used to have a strong current, and now there's just a trickle of water left. How are we going to be able to plant?... We're going to have to fight hard... and not for us, but to pass it on to our children, and our grandchildren'. (Barcellos & Batista Ferreira, 2008)

Companies engaged in agribusiness and resource extraction have used multiple tactics to grab land, including deceptive certification processes and co-optation of community members through the creation of groups of 'independent producers.' These groups have been acting against the collective claims of their own communities. Many of those peasant Indigenous women and men who were driven into selling their lands through deceptive strategies were incorporated into an exploitative labour system which has taken a heavy toll on their socioeconomic emancipation and their identity as Q'eqchi' peoples (Fradejas, 2013). In Colombia, land grabbing has also entailed violent evictions of peasant communities, with the government privileging large-scale investment from national and foreign companies. These companies have occupied a large part of the land that should have been redistributed in line with the government's commitments to equitable land redistribution. This was a key point in the Colombian Peace Accords Agenda and women peacemakers fought hard to have this right incorporated into the official text of the 2016 Peace Accord. In the Brazilian region of Maranhão, violence has escalated, with human rights groups recording a spate of land conflicts targeting Indigenous people and rural workers, even after they had relocated to find refuge from death threats related to land conflicts (Ennes, 2021).

Impacts on women's bodies and their sexual and reproductive health rights

Large-scale agribusiness and extractive activities rely heavily on the use of pesticides and chemicals. These toxic elements have proven to be extremely harmful to women's and men's health. In Chile, ANAMURI, which is part of the autonomous international peasant food sovereignty movement Via Campesina,[1] have been denouncing and documenting the impacts of pesticides on women's health since 2009. They have collected robust evidence from women rural workers and migrant seasonal workers (*temporeras*) demonstrating that the chemicals used by companies engaged in agribusiness for fruit export are a threat to theirs and their children's health:

> 'Since I was a child I have worked in the fields harvesting fruit, and now I work in export companies... chemicals against pests are a constant fear, as I have seen many colleagues with their bodies burned by being sprayed with pesticides... many today have skin cancer... after being poisoned with chemicals I got informed and I know that by law the companies must give me the tools for risk prevention against pesticides'. (ANAMURI, no date)

Evidence also includes testimonies from young pregnant women workers who reported an increase in the number of miscarriages and congenital malformations due to the use of pesticides.

Echoing ANAMURI, as early as 2012, international Indigenous women's networks were already presenting alarming evidence in international policymaking spaces. Participants including women from Latin America and the Caribbean in the first International Indigenous Women's Environmental and Reproductive Health Symposium stated that Indigenous peoples, specifically women and children, were suffering the 'detrimental, devastating, multi-generational and deadly impacts' of environmental contaminants, including: the contamination of mothers' breast milk; disproportionate levels of reproductive system cancers, including in young people; increasing numbers of miscarriages and stillbirths; and high levels of sterility and infertility (UN, 2010).

In Brazil, the heavy use of chemicals has also had a negative impact on the health of women workers in large-scale oil palm plantations. In a survey made in Baixo Jaguaribe, a region of the Ceará state in North-eastern Brazil, women identified multiple effects on their bodies, including throat and eye irritations, impact on their respiratory system, repetitive strain injury (RSI), increased occurrences of cancer cases, cases of congenital malformation and 'early puberty'. These are all health problems which have grown exponentially since the arrival of agribusiness companies in the area. Impacts on women's mental health were also mentioned, as women workers have had to cope with the traumatizing experience of land dispossession, exposure to pesticides and chemicals, exploitative working conditions, and sexual and gender violence (Melo & Rigotto, 2018).

In Colombia, chemicals used in land grabbed for oil palm plantations have contaminated rivers which are key to ensuring communities' wellbeing and food security. As a result, women have no other choice but to cook with the contaminated water, and communities have to drink the poisoned water with negative consequences for their health, such as vomiting, fever, skin irritations, and stomach problems. The harmful effects of pesticides are compellingly described by Catalina (fictitious name), a local Afro-descendant woman leader in María la Baja rural zone in northern Colombia:

> 'This land was abundant. Now there is nothing left, because the land has been planted with palm, and there are plagues... the water is contaminated by the agrochemicals they put in the palm: that is why all the women have vaginal infections, there are many skin diseases, especially in the children, and also kidney diseases'. (Castro, 2018:15)

In rural areas, and particularly in Indigenous and Afro-descendant territories, communities use the water that comes from the mountain peaks for productive work and reproductive care (cooking healthy food for their families, ensuring cleanliness, hygiene, and prevention of epidemics such as cholera). Therefore, grabbing water and rivers for large-scale and export-driven agribusiness is a violation of fundamental human rights, both individual and collective: the right to life; to an adequate standard of living, and to the highest attainable standards of physical and mental wellbeing.

Land grabbing is also a major cause of physical and sexual violence against women, particularly visible at the moment in which communities are evicted from their land. 'They left me completely battered, like a crushed orange,' stated an Indigenous Maya-Q'eqchis woman who survived rape at the hands of police and security forces during the forced expulsion of her community in 2007, in territories claimed by the Canadian HudBay Minerals mining company in Guatemala. 'It hurts to remember what happened that day... I lost my baby because of what all those men did to me,' another survivor of the Lote Ocho tragedy shared.[2] The presence of extractive projects - often the reason behind land grabbing - is also associated with an increase in gender violence, for example in cases of prostitution, trafficking of women and children, and harassment, and rape (Solano Ortíz, 2015).

Land grabbing and extractivism are undeniable root causes and catalysts of violence against women's bodies and violate women's fundamental human rights (social, economic, political, cultural, sexual, and reproductive) as well as the right to live and produce in a non-polluted environment. In this sense, land grabbing is directly linked to environmental violence and is inextricable from women's sexual and reproductive health rights.

In the everyday lives of women in territories affected by land grabbing, intersectional gender-based violence manifests itself not only in the harm done directly to their bodies, but also in the harm done to Nature. This includes violent acts such as the intentional burning of forests that are key to their survival, and the contamination of soil and depletion of watersheds, rivers, and oceans which ensure their livelihoods and sexual and reproductive health rights. Environmental violence is therefore strongly connected to women's bodily and psychological integrity. This specific connection has been defined by Indigenous women leaders in Argentina as 'terricide' (*terricidio*): the killing of all forms of life - including Nature (ecocide), women (femicide/feminicide), and Indigenous peoples (genocide). Many groups explicitly highlight this link between harm to Mother Earth and harm to women - like ANAMURI (2017): 'We, the women of ANAMURI, say loud and clear that violence against biodiversity and our Mother Earth is also capitalist and patriarchal violence against women', and Nina Gualinga, an Indigenous Kichwa activist from Sarayaku in the Ecuadorian Amazon: 'As Indigenous women we're protecting our territories. We're protecting the mountains, the forest, the water, the air, and our bodies are part of the land. Any violation of our land is a violation of our bodies' (Morales De la Cruz, 2022). This concept has been politicized in Ecuador and Bolivia as *Sumak Kawsay* (see Box 4.1).

Box 4.1: *Sumak Kawsay*/Buen Vivir (Living Well)

'For me, taking care of the territories is associated with taking care of nature and the environment... but above all, it is about taking care of the common good... to take care of our Buen Vivir'. (Viviana Catrileo, ANAMURI, Chile)

Sumak Kawsay is an Indigenous Kichwa philosophy based on the communion of humans and nature in harmonious existence, often described as 'Living Well', in English, and 'Buen Vivir' in Spanish. It posits the rights of people and the rights of Mother Earth on equal terms, so harm done to one is harm done to the other. Although an Andean concept, similar cosmovisions exist within other Indigenous communities in Chile, Paraguay, Brazil, and other countries in Latin America.

The rights of Nature were enshrined in the national Constitutions of Ecuador (2008) and Bolivia (2010). Both Constitutions declare Pachamama (Mother Earth) as a subject entitled to the right to integral respect. In addition to giving nature rights, Ecuador's Constitution also gives its people the right to resist activities or processes that threaten their Constitutional rights. These include the right to a safe environment, and the right to *Sumak Kawsay*. In Bolivia, the first Rights of Nature statute came into effect in 2010. The Law of the Rights of Mother Earth states that Pachamama is a dynamic living system with legal personality, and that it is considered sacred, according to the cosmovision of Indigenous original peoples and peasant communities. The statute also declares that any Bolivian may bring a legal action on Nature's behalf. A second law adopted in 2012 establishes an enforceable right to climate justice, which can be brought by victims of climate change who have been denied the right to *Sumak Kawsay* (International Rivers, 2020).

Despite these transformative policy initiatives, the *Sumak Kawsay* principles have not been enforced and land grabbing has continued unabated in these countries, with governments failing to protect the rights of Nature and neglecting to enforce legal measures to protect rural Indigenous people's customary land rights. Lack of enforcement of *Sumak Kawsay* principles has led women to engage in resistance strategies. While enshrined in the philosophy of *Sumak Kawsay*, these strategies tend to emphasize the normative dimension of the state's obligation to redistribute land and territory – in line with national land tenure legislation, and the individual and collective dimension of land rights – rather than actual practices of Buen Vivir.

Sources: Cárdenas (2020), Cyrus R. Vance Centre for International Justice, Earth Law Centre and International Rivers (2020)

Geopolitical aspect of land grabbing

It is important to consider the geopolitical dimension of land grabbing-related violence, especially in the ways it has affected Indigenous people. The struggle of Indigenous peoples is an example of historical resistance against colonial power relations and capitalist-driven interests, which have for centuries exerted different forms of violence on their bodies and ecosystems. Land grabbing-related violence is, this sense, a consequence of geopolitical arrangements between patriarchal states and corporate businesses to control markets and territories for profit maximization. These geopolitical arrangements assume access to land and territories as commodities rather than fundamental human rights. Resisting the geopolitics of violence inflicted on the bodies and territories of Indigenous and peasant women, and reclaiming the right to Buen Vivir and food sovereignty has brought together peasant and Indigenous women in Brazil.

> 'The Indigenous cause cannot be erased from history by the "victors"; it is necessary that we remember it... because it is a struggle of unity and strength that restores the principles of the collective struggle, of protection of our greatest assets that are configured in territory, nature, life, identities, and without which we do not exist. We reaffirm our commitment to weaving together the network of sustainability and solidarity for Living Well. But we also reaffirm that there is no Living Well when there are tears and blood coming from women violated in our peasant communities and traditional peoples due to the oppressive system, patriarchy, and machismo.' (ANMC, 2021: 12)

Women resisting land grabbing and environmental violence

Through international campaigns, women leaders have spoken out against land grabbing for the ways it perpetuates systemic violence and accentuates the dispossession and vulnerability of rural communities, specifically endangering the lives of the next generations and their right to food sovereignty.

Many women all over Latin America are resisting land grabbing under the principle of *Sumak Kawsay* – through social care activities within their communities which promote Living Well, and also through mobilizing their communities, participating in politics, and organizing popular assemblies and consultations. For example, Mujeres Amazónicas is a collective of over 100 (mostly Indigenous) women from six Indigenous nations across the Ecuadorian Amazon, who fight to protect Indigenous women's rights, alleviate gender-based violence, defend their territories against land grabbers, protect the environment, education, and health, and preserve their cultural traditions from generation to generation. Their work is heavily informed by the concept of *Sumak Kawsay*. Campaigns include a petition for justice for María Taant, a Shuar leader from the Ecuadorian Amazon who vocally resisted the occupation of her territory and body, fought for her four children, and was killed in a suspicious hit-and-run incident. They recently opened an Amazonian Women's House in Puya, where women congregate to take part in cultural and educational activities.[3]

Many rural and Indigenous women, for example those of ANAMURI, have embraced food sovereignty as a form of resistance that is inclusive of Nature's rights and promotes non-violent modes of production. The principle of food sovereignty was coined by Via Campesina in 1996 and it implies the right of a country to produce in an autonomous way, deciding on the type of food that it produces and ensuring the right to adequate and healthy food for all (Via Campesina, 2003). This resistance paradigm is crucial for peasant and rural women in Latin America since it implies caring for local ecosystems and biodiversity and ensuring access to healthy and adequate food for local communities and local markets. The adoption of food sovereignty has also led to rural women's empowerment, with ANAMURI successfully influencing agrarian policies in their struggle against pesticides and GMO (genetically modified organisms).

Women are also responding by implementing sustainable agricultural practices that ensure the protection and conservation of ecosystems and communities. One of these models is agroecology, through which women have been able to ensure food security and food sovereignty, self-sustenance, income generation, and environmental protection. The peasant women's movement (MMC) in Brazil, for example, advocates for the protection of agroecological peasant agriculture. This model is based on diversification and sustainable agricultural systems, producing crops that guarantee food sovereignty for the family and consumers, and protect natural resources. In the Brazilian Amazon, Indigenous women leaders have also ensured protection and conservation of local ecosystems through preserving and passing on their ancestral knowledge to communities. Edilena Krikati has been advocating for the sovereignty of women's bodies, lands, and territories, collecting evidence on the harm done by land grabbing and proposing alternatives that protect them and their ecosystems. Edilena says:

> 'We women are the first to feel and observe the impacts and changes related to climate in our daily lives because we have a special relationship with nature and territory. We are also the ones who save the seeds and pass on this and other knowledge to new generations, including the different ways of doing territorial protection'. (Bonilha, 2019)

Amazonian women leaders in Maranhão have implemented agroecological solutions such as protecting seeds and ecosystems through reforestation, creating nurseries with native seeds and medicinal plants, beekeeping and producing honey, organizing seed exchanges, revitalizing rivers and springs, organizing fire brigades, and caring for spirituality and the continuous and permanent protection of Mother Earth, her waters and forests (Bonilha, 2019).

In Peru, for example, the National Organization of Andean and Amazonian Women (ONAMIAP) are advocating for policies that would ensure women's land rights and sustainable food security in conflict mitigation, including conservation practices of their ecosystems in Indigenous and Afro-descendant territories. In Paraguay, women of the Qom people have been producing for their communities and local markets in ways that protect biodiversity. This includes using their ancestral knowledge on protection and preservation of biodiversity and defending their right to a clean environment, including non-polluted water for productive and reproductive work. They've built a well in order to access potable water in an area being dried out by eucalyptus monoculture. They are also preserving and reforesting *totora*, a native plant similar to the bulrush, that grows in pools of water and collects rainwater, as well as being used artisanally (Fajardo, 2021).

However, women's activism against environmental violence risks further gendered violence against them, once again showing the inextricable link between environmental violence and violence against women. At the grassroots, women leaders have for many years systematically denounced the gendered and intersecting forms of violence impinging on them because they are women. Berta Cáceres, who worked defending the territory and rights of her fellow Lenca people in Honduras, is widely quoted as saying:

> 'It's not easy to be a woman leading Indigenous resistance strategies. In an incredibly patriarchal society, we women are incredibly vulnerable, we have to deal with extremely risky situations, and misogynistic, machista campaigns.'

Like other environmental activists in their struggles against state and corporate-driven violence, Berta was confronted with everyday forms of violence ranging from surveillance, harassment, death threats, and criminalization, and she was eventually murdered (see Box 4.2).

Box 4.2: Berta Cáceres

Berta Cáceres was a prominent Indigenous environmental leader, and the world-renowned recipient of the 2015 Goldman Environmental Prize for her work defending the territory and rights of the Lenca people in Honduras. In 1993 she co-founded the Civic Council of Indigenous and Popular Organizations (Consejo Cívico de Organizaciones Indígenas Populares – COPINH), with whom she led campaigns against dam projects that would cut off food and water supplies to Indigenous communities. Berta led strategies including filing complaints with government authorities, bringing local community representatives to meetings in the Honduran capital, Tegucigalpa, organizing local assemblies where community members could vote against harmful projects, and leading protests to peacefully demand a voice. Berta also reached out to the international community and managed to bring cases to international courts.

On 3 March 2016, she was brutally murdered by two men who broke into her home in the city of Esperanza. In December 2019, seven men were convicted of her murder (three of them linked to the military), but prosecution of the intellectual authors is still pending, and unreasonable delays have been permitted by the judiciary. In June 2022, Roberto David Castillo, whose company had been awarded the contract to build the Zarza dam which Cácaeres was leading a campaign against, was sentenced to over 22 years in jail for planning Berta's murder and hiring the gunmen. The energy executive is a former president of Honduran power company, Desa, and a US-trained former Honduran army intelligence officer. However, as stated by Cáceres' family and in an official document of the USA Congress, there is evidence that members of the Honduran elite were responsible for ordering Cáceres's assassination, and that these intellectual authors remain in impunity. Evidence also indicates the possible involvement of military officials of high rank, who are not currently being investigated.

Sources: COPINH (2021), Congress.gov (2021)

Figure 4.1: Berta Cáceres, 2015 Goldman Environmental Award Recipient. Credit: coolloud

Tackling impunity

In light of the intensification of land grabbing and its disenfranchising impacts on women's human rights and on environmental sustainability, women's organizations and networks have been systematically raising awareness and mobilizing constituencies at the local, national, and international level. At the political level, they have highlighted the urgency of implementing laws and policies that (re)distribute land equitably, while calling upon governments to stop the culture of impunity surrounding land grabbing-related violence against women, girls, and trans persons.

> 'The protection of our health, lands, resources... and our traditional knowledge... are inherent and inalienable human rights. These rights are affirmed in the UN Declaration on the Rights of Indigenous Peoples and other international standards, and must be upheld, respected, and fully implemented.' (UN, 2010)

Women have stressed the government's duty to enforce existing legislation and hold companies and private sector actors accountable for any infringement of women's right to a life free from violence, including land dispossession, forced displacement, and poisoning of their ecosystems. As duty bearers, public institutions (including the judiciary) and private actors (including companies) are accountable for acting with due diligence. Lack of action by governments is a form of state violence that needs to be considered as an act of non-assistance to persons in danger.

With support from civil society organizations (CSOs), many Indigenous women leaders have documented the intensification of domestic violence in private spaces and structural violence in territories and protected areas disputed by agribusiness and extractive companies. They have denounced the increased intentional burning of their lands, homes, and communities; violent occupations of their lands and territories; forced displacement; and governments' reluctance to take action. Many have also denounced the impunity surrounding killings of rural, peasant, Indigenous and Afro-descendant land rights defenders like Berta Cáceres.

Edilena Krikati is among women grassroots leaders who have condemned the racial dimension of land grabbing and institutionalized impunity in cases of violence against Indigenous women. She has stated that racial prejudice is so strong in Brazil that people no longer hide their prejudice against Indigenous peoples: 'We are now perceiving more clearly this prejudice that was hidden before. Before people disguised it well; today they don't. It is normal for people to say that they don't like Indians.' (Brigada NINJA Amazônia, 2019). Krikati's testimony is supported by overwhelming evidence that in today's Brazil, cases of land grabbing-related violence against Indigenous people are often met with impunity. In 2019, 31 people were killed in a wave of rural violence that activists argue was driven by the Brazilian government's anti-Indigenous rhetoric. Mongabay reporter Daniel Camargos states (2021):

> 'When Jair Bolsonaro took office as president of Brazil at the start of 2019, he ushered in a climate of hostility toward rural activists - Indigenous peoples, environmentalists, advocates for landless workers' rights, and communities subsisting off the sustainable extraction of forest resources.'

Most of those killed were defending their territories at the time, and many of them were affiliated with landless workers' or Indigenous people's movements. There have been no convictions, and police investigations into 19 of the murders continue today, with no answers. The sole case that has been closed was ruled an accidental drowning, despite 'evidence of violence against the Indigenous victim'.

Reluctance on the part of public authorities to enforce existing legislation in cases of land grabbing-related violence has exacerbated vulnerability and forced women leaders to organize themselves to ensure protection of their lives, lands, and ecosystems. The inhabitants of protected areas in Maranhão, for example, have been made more vulnerable as the federal government refuses to comply with its duty to protect Indigenous lands. Indigenous people in Maranhão have been forced to organize themselves. They monitor and protect their lands and identify and report criminal activities and violations carried out by hunters, loggers, drug traffickers and other invaders. But, as Patrícia Bonilha of Greenpeace Brazil points out, this badly needed work has also increased their chances of falling victim to violence (Bonilha, 2019).

Eloy Terena, Indigenous lawyer and legal advisor to the Coordination of the Indigenous Organizations of the Brazilian Amazon (COIAB), states:

> 'Dealing with the absence of the State is part of our day-to-day reality. We use our vehicles to monitor and survey our lands, putting our lives at risk. What's left of the Amazon biome is on our lands and we have preserved it very well. This is part of our struggle and it's the reason we are exposed to threats from farmers, miners and even politicians.' (Hivos, 2021)

Described as an international bill of rights for women, CEDAW is an international treaty adopted in 1979 by the United Nations General Assembly. Nineteen Latin American countries have ratified the bill, which guarantees women's right to a life free from violence. This means they are legally bound to put its provisions into practice, and they are committed to submitting national reports at least every four years on measures they have taken to comply with their obligations. CEDAW's General Recommendation 34 on rural women stipulates that 'Rural women human rights defenders are often at risk of violence when working, for example, to protect victims, transform local customs or secure natural resource rights.' It also states that rural women are overrepresented among agricultural workers in many regions, 'exposing them to increased health risks linked to the improper and extensive use of fertilizers and pesticides by various actors, resulting in illnesses, early deaths, pregnancy complications, foetal disorders, and physical and developmental disorders in infants and children.' (CEDAW, 2016:14)

Recommendation 34 calls upon state parties to:

> 'Implement measures to prevent and address threats and attacks against rural women human rights defenders, with particular attention to those engaged on issues relating to land and natural resources, women's health, including sexual and reproductive rights, the elimination of discriminatory customs and practices, and gender-based violence.' (CEDAW, 2016:8)

> 'Establish quotas and targets for rural women's representation in decision-making positions, specifically in parliaments and governance bodies at all levels, including in land, forestry, fishery and water governance bodies, as well as natural resource management.' (CEDAW, 2016:16)

> 'Ensure that legislation guarantees rural women's rights to land, water and other natural resources on an equal basis with men... They should ensure that Indigenous women in rural areas have equal access with Indigenous men to ownership and possession of and control over land, water, forests, fisheries, aquaculture and other resources that they have traditionally owned, occupied or otherwise used or acquired, including by protecting them against discrimination and dispossession.' (CEDAW, 2016:16-17)

Yet despite CEDAW's recommendations, several countries in the region have disregarded obligations related to equitable land

---

Box 4.3: ILO Convention No. 169 'Towards an inclusive, sustainable and just future'

This ILO Convention stipulates that any natural resource that will be extracted from Indigenous land and territories (owned or claimed) needs to be first engaged in a genuine process of free, prior and informed consultation with affected communities. The principle driving ILO Convention 169 is that consultation must occur 'in order to obtain the free, prior and informed consent' of affected Indigenous peoples. This principle was also incorporated in the 2007 UN Declaration on the Rights of Indigenous Peoples.

Source: UN (2007)

---

distribution and have instead prioritized the interests of large-scale land investments. In Brazil, for example, the government has not complied with its obligation to restore ancestral land to Indigenous and Afro-descendant peoples (Quilombolas).[4] In Colombia, the government has failed to restore land to women and men displaced by the armed conflict. As shown throughout this chapter, governments' responses and mechanisms to prevent and punish violence against rural women human rights defenders – with particular attention to those engaged on issues relating to land and natural resources – have been weak.

Similarly, the Beijing Declaration and the Platform for Action is a global policy agenda for women's empowerment and gender equality, adopted unanimously by 189 countries in 1995, including all countries in Latin America and the Caribbean. Although not a binding instrument (countries are free to implement recommendations or not, and can choose to report or not), governments following the declaration have committed to ensuring that women's economic activities – traditional and new – are not affected by national policies related to international and regional trade agreements [Paragraph 165, k] and that 'All enterprises, including transnational corporations, comply with national laws and codes, social security standards, existing international agreements, instruments and conventions, including those relating to the environment, and other relevant laws' [Paragraph 165, l.] (UN, 1995:69). The declaration is clearly being ignored throughout the region.

Women influencing do-no-harm policies and practices

Developed in the 1990s, Do No Harm (DNH) is an approach which aims to prevent NGOs working in conflict and post-conflict settings from causing unintended negative consequences. Women's power for influencing DNH policies and practices has been amply demonstrated. For example, the International Indigenous Women's Forum (IIWF/FIMI) has been advocating and lobbying for DNH policies and practices since their creation. Their work is sustained by Indigenous women at the grassroots and nourished by their ancestral knowledge and experiences, with special emphasis on defending their fundamental human rights both as women, and as constitutive members of Indigenous groups. FIMI has exposed the systemic and intersecting nature of violence against Indigenous women in several UN Fora (CEDAW, CSW, FAO, COOP 26) and has allied with CSOs such as the International Land Coalition. To FIMI, structural violence against women and girls is not only gender-based, but also intersectional. This means that it is rooted in a colonial past, has been fueled by racism, and exacerbated by patriarchal capitalism. FIMI defines the drivers of structural violence against Indigenous women as:

> 'Macroeconomic adjustment policies that affect Indigenous women disproportionally; discriminatory laws related to land rights, natural resources, loans and credit; aggressive development projects such as mining and agribusiness on Indigenous land which result in land contamination, dispossession and loss of traditional livelihood assets.' (FIMI, 2020:13)

FIMI has also documented the plight of Indigenous women migrants whose lived experience of migration from rural to urban areas has often been the result of land dispossession, food insecurity, and conflict-related forced displacement. Throughout their political and conceptual work, they have redefined violence against women in ways that include the macro and the micro level of gendered intersectional VAWG: at the macro level, intersecting violences resulting from land grabbing include structural discrimination, institutional racism, corporate and state violence. Micro violences are those that are part of women's everyday life. They take place in private and public spaces and are often naturalized or condoned (verbal, physical, psychological, sexual, economic, patrimonial, spiritual). Indigenous women have conceptualized systemic and micro-level violences (in plural) as inextricable from each other, where the violence experienced as individual women is inseparable from the violence exerted on their peoples and territories, including ecosystems'. (FIMI 2006; FIMI 2021; ECMIA 2021)

FIMI has also done advocacy work at the international level. In 2021, the United Nations CEDAW Committee launched a civil society consultation process aimed at receiving inputs to include in a new General Recommendation on Indigenous women and girls (known as Recommendation #39, although not yet adopted).[5] FIMI and MADRE, an organization with which they work closely on international advocacy, made a submission to the Committee. In it, FIMI draws attention to the fact that 'CEDAW does not specifically recognize Indigenous Women and Girls [sic] as bearers of individual and collective rights.' FIMI also stresses the systemic and intersectional nature of the violence endured by Indigenous women and girls inside and outside their territories and calls upon the State in its role as duty bearer to 'address the consequences of historic injustices and to provide support and reparations to the affected communities as part of reconciliation and the process of building societies free from discrimination against indigenous women and girls', including urban, rural, older, displaced, refugee, migrant, LGBTQ+ Indigenous women; as well as those in situations of poverty and those with disabilities (FIMI, 2021:6)

It also demands that states collect disaggregated data on the forms of gender-based discrimination and violence faced by Indigenous women and girls.

FIMI's input highlights the importance of enforcing existing international frameworks to ensure prevention of gendered and intersectional VAWG, protection to victims and survivors of VAWG, and punishment of public and private actors who fail to act with due diligence in cases of land grabbing-related VAWG:

> 'The dispossession and usurpation of indigenous lands and territories without their free, prior, and informed consent deprives indigenous women and girls of livelihood sources which are vital for their survival; creates unsafe conditions for them; and facilitates the incursion of state and non-state actors which often commit violence against them.' (FIMI, 2021:7)

In 2019, the CEDAW Committee was also targeted by organizations and networks of rural and peasant women. In alliance with Colombian CSOs and with support from the International Land Coalition, they submitted a shadow report to the CEDAW Committee. This was the first report focusing on the specific challenges affecting rural and peasant women in Colombia. Key issues highlighted in the report were the need for the government to enforce its commitments regarding equality in land restitution (as stipulated in the Peace Agreements), to include the specific needs of rural and peasant women, and to effectively guarantee their participation in processes related to restitution, remedy, and protection (CEDAW, 2019).

Influencing policies through case laws

Following similar resistance pathways, in the highlands of Atacama, Northern Chile, Indigenous women of the Colla Pai Ote people have been mobilizing to challenge the recent decision by the Chilean government to open their territory to foreign investment for resource extraction (lithium). They are using the International Labour Organization (ILO) Convention 169, a binding instrument, to sue the State.

The government's plan is to open 80,000 hectares of land rich in natural resources for lithium extraction, in order to reactivate the country's economy after the COVID-19 pandemic. This threatens the Colla Pai Ote people's food sovereignty and their ecosystems. Together with their male peers, the Colla women have openly contested the government's decision and are doing strong media, advocacy, and lobbying work to raise awareness on the possible impacts of this new wave of land grabbing in their territories. Recently, they filed an appeal in the local court of Copiapó, in the Atacama region, as the lands that were selected for foreign resource extraction are part of the Colla ancestral territories, a region they have inhabited even before Spanish colonizers came more than five centuries ago. In their ancestral lands, they have been able to ensure the sustainable livelihoods of their communities, generate income through sustainable farming practices, and protect the local ecosystems, which include Salt Lakes. Their key contention is that their right to due and proper consent, as recommended by the ILO Convention 169, has not been respected by the government.

In an interview in January 2022, Ercilia Araya, a well-known Colla Pai Ote woman leader, local producer, and livestock (goat) pastoralist, explains why she is leading a movement on behalf of Indigenous peoples across the north of Chile:

> 'We are pastoralists. Some of us raise cattle (goats) and make cheese for local consumption; others do farming and small-scale mining. We live and produce in harmony with our Mother Earth. We follow our ancestral model of production and development which ensures protection of our biodiversity. The impact of land grabbing for lithium extraction will be devastating to our communities and our ecosystem: land and water will be grabbed, including areas that should be protected by the State, such as the Maricunga Salt Lake. Water will be grabbed by the companies and riverbeds will be polluted, the air will be polluted, the soil will be contaminated. Our traditional routes to reach green pastures for our cattle will be closed, access to our ancestral holy sites will be blocked, our means of self-sustenance will be destroyed. The harm done to our people and our Mother Earth needs to be prevented. This is state violence that we are experiencing: we have been denied our right to our ancestral lands and territories and we have been forced to rent plots of land situated

Figure 4.2: Ercilia Araya at the first panel on human rights violations against Indigenous people during the dictatorship. Credit: Observatorio Ciudadano/YouTube

in our ancestral territories. These plots are owned by families in the mining business who do not live here. We were denied our right to be informed and to proper consultation, as indicated by the ILO Convention 169. This is why we took the government to Court.' (Ercilia Araya, 2022)

On 14 February 2022, the court gave a positive response and received the Appeal, invoking ILO Convention 169 and constitutional principles (Minga, 2022). This is a landmark victory which shows women's power for influencing decisions that can be harmful to their bodies, territories, communities, and ecosystems.

Women across Latin America are successfully demonstrating that the expansion of land grabbing has gone hand in hand with serious human rights violations, and they have in many cases successfully pressured governments through DNH policies and case laws. However, substantive challenges remain before governments agree to ensure caring economies and laws which guarantee women's fundamental right to a life free from all forms of VAWG – including land-grabbing related violence. Notably, under COVID-19 lockdown rules, it became more difficult for women to denounce land grabbing-related violence against them, given decreased mobility, court closures, and increased everyday violence against women.

Land grabbing-related violence during the pandemic

During the COVID-19 lockdown land grabbing worsened with rural, peasant, Indigenous, and Afro-descendant land rights defenders being particularly targeted – by illegal miners, loggers, and staff from big companies engaged in agribusiness and resource extraction. The pandemic allowed them to threaten communities, and grab or burn resources which communities rely on like water, plots of land, and forests. COVID-19 mobility restrictions, lockdowns, and travel bans further hindered women land rights defenders from seeking and obtaining protection, going into hiding, or finding other places of safety. As the examples below show, in some countries, such as Brazil and Chile, governments have even loosened environmental restrictions, opening territories rich in natural resources to big businesses. The plight of women and men in territories disputed by land grabbers is in fact a 'triple pandemic' which includes health inequities, a dramatic increase in deforestation and forest fires, and growing violence against women and men who are struggling against land grabbing (Bolaños, 2020).

Evidence collected by human rights organizations confirms the pandemic of violence affecting human rights and land rights defenders in Latin America. During 2019, an average of four land and environmental defenders were killed in the region *every week*, with high levels of corporation-related attacks. In 2020, at least 331 human rights defenders were killed (287 men, 38 women, and four trans people). A majority of the leaders killed (69 per cent) were human rights defenders working on land, Indigenous peoples, and environmental rights. 28 per cent were working on women's rights and 26 per cent were working specifically on Indigenous peoples' rights (FLD, 2021).

Regarding the specific plight of rural women, a recent report by the UN-FAO shows that the COVID-19 pandemic further restricted rural women's mobility. Mobility is key for rural women to be able to sell their products in local markets, but the pandemic brought the closure of markets and interruption of their supply chains. These constraints have been compounded by gender-based violence at home, and barriers in accessing productive resources such as land, water, and agricultural inputs (FAO/AECDI, 2021).

Conclusions

Across the continent, women have been weaving powers and building a collective chain of voices to resist land grabbing and denounce its everyday forms of violence – against the environment, women, and communities. Through social care activities, campaigning, advocacy, and lobbying at regional, national, and international levels, women are making their voices heard. Their resistance has gone hand in hand with an urgent call for governments and big businesses (including transnational companies) to stop harming their bodies, lands, and territories.

Their struggles bear witness to women's power to resist, mobilize, and propose sustainable and caring alternatives to the gendered and intersecting forms of violence generated by land grabbing and resource extraction. In many countries, their struggles have been met with violence and rampant impunity. Women are critically aware that the struggle against land grabbing and resource extraction is political, territorial, and environmental. Their message is loud and clear: governments have the obligation to prevent all forms of violence against women, girls, and trans persons - both within and outside of territories disputed by big corporations - through enforcement of existing legislation and in line with international commitments.

Finally, women's struggle against the violence generated by land grabbing is also geopolitical. It involves struggling against structural intersectional discrimination in the distribution of wealth and resources, and strategic negotiations in private and public spaces for women's empowerment and political agency. For Indigenous, Afro descendant, and rural women, access to land rights means acquiring the power to exert their fundamental human rights at the individual, community, and household level. On a larger scale, it means reclaiming a development model based on social justice and fundamental freedoms; a model generated under dignifying and equitable conditions.

Saying NO to oil palm, NO to violence, NO to taking our lives—and they kill us not just with bullets, but also by taking away our lands and territories.

Because this is not afforestation, it is deforestation.Because this is not work, it is slavery.This is not life, it is death.

Today we raise our voices, united and empowered, and we say ENOUGH IS ENOUGH!

Poem by Flor Contreras Ulloa, Honduras. (World Rainforest Movement, 2021)

Notes

1. La Via Campesina (LVC) was founded in 1986. LVC is an autonomous international movement made up of over 200 million peasants, small-scale farmers, landless peoples, farmworkers, Indigenous Peoples, and other food producers from around 70 countries. LVC struggles for food sovereignty, a term they coined and which they define as the peoples' right over their food systems, their right to produce nutritious food for

communities everywhere, and their right to develop and apply culturally appropriate models of agricultural production.
2. The lawsuit of the women from Lote Ocho in Guatemala has made history. Since its filing in 2007, other Canadian mining companies have been sued for negligence in Canada for alleged human rights violations committed abroad. The full story of the Lote Ocho case can be found at https://newint.org/features/2021/10/07/our-whole-truth-will-come-out-canada.
3. The group regularly post campaign images and information to their Instagram page @mujeresamazonicas
4. For more on why land demarcation is important for Indigenous and Quilombola women, see Raízes (2018)
5. In November 2021, the CEDAW Committee agreed that the next General Recommendation (#39) would be focused on the rights of Indigenous Women and Girls. Consultation with civil society organizations was part of a participatory process to bring this recommendation close to Indigenous women's specific needs and priorities. The official adoption process is still pending.

Bibliography

Alonso-Fradejas, A. (2013) 'Land & sovereignty in the Americas', *TNI*, issue brief 1, https://www.tni.org/files/download/land-sov_series_briefs_-_ndeg1_alonso-fradejas_final.pdf

ANAMURI Chile (no date), 'Pesticides. Radio topic 34', https://www.anamuri.cl/cu%C3%B1as

ANAMURI (2017) 'Yo no elegí ser sacrificable...calama: zona de sacrificio', Tribunal Ético Calama, Chile, Sábado 29 de octubre, Sede de la CUT de Calama, Vargas #2201, https://www.anamuri.cl/copia-de-semilla

ANMC - Associação Nacional de Mulheres Camponesas (2021). *FEMINISMO CAMPESINO POPULAR Reflexiones a partir de experiencias en el Movimiento de Mujeres Campesinas de Brasil (MMC)*. 1st ed en español. Passo Fundo, https://bizilur.eus/wp-content/uploads/2021/10/FEMINISMO-CAMPESINO-POPULAR_MMC-BRASIL-ESP.pdf

Araya, E. (2022), interviewed by Patricia Muñoz Cabrera, 21 January

Barcellos, G.H. and Batista Ferreira, S. (2008) 'Women and eucalyptus: stories of life and resistance', *World Rainforest Movement*, https://www.wrm.org.uy//wp-content/uploads/2013/02/Book_Women.pdf

Bolaños, O. (2020) 'Latin America's indigenous and afro-descendant women face a "triple pandemic"', https://news.trust.org/item/20200709182830-27m6r

Bonilha, P. (2019) 'Mulheres indígenas debatem mudanças climáticas para garantir proteção territorial', *BiodiversidadLA*, https://www.biodiversidadla.org/Noticias/Mulheres-indigenas-debatemmudancas-climaticas-para-garantir-protecao-territorial

Brigada, N.A., Galvão, R. and Flávio L. (2019) 'Edilena Krikati: "As pessoas não disfarçam mais o preconceito contra indígenas"', *Midia Ninja*, https://brigada.midianinja.org/edilena-krikati-aspessoas-nao-disfarcam-mais-o-preconceito-contra-indigenas

Cárdenas, K. (2020) 'Resistir: mujeres rurales en contra del extractivismo (el caso de ANAMURI, Chile)', *BiodiversidadLA*, https://www.biodiversidadla.org/Multimedia/Video/Resistir-mujeres-rurales-en-contra-del-extractivismo-el-caso-de-ANAMURI-Chile

Camargos, D. (2021) 'Zero convictions as impunity blocks justice for victims of Brazil's rural violence', *Mongabay*, https://news.mongabay.com/2021/02/zero-convictions-as-impunity-blocks-justice-for-victims-of-brazils-rural-violence

Castro, N. (2018) 'IN Boletín Nº 236 del WRM', *WRM*, March, https://www.wrm.org.uy//es/files/2018/03/Bolet%c3%adn-236_ESP.pdf

CEDAW (2016) 'Convention on the elimination of all forms of discrimination against women. General recommendation No. 34 (2016) on the rights of rural women', https://tbinternet.ohchr.org/_layouts/15/treatybodyexternal/TBSearch.aspx?Lang=en&TreatyID=3&DocTypeID=11>

CEDAW (2019) 'Primer informe sombra específico de mujeres rurales y campesinas en Colombia', https://d3o3cb4w253x5q.cloudfront.net/media/documents/infoalternomcr-07.pdf

Congress.gov. Text – H.R.1574 – 117th Congress (2021-2022), 'Berta Cáceres Human Rights in Honduras Act', 3 March, https://www.congress.gov/bill/117th-congress/house-bill/1574/text

Copinh (2021) 'Honduras: agentes estatales implicados en asesinato de Berta Cáceres', https://berta.copinh.org/tag/gaipe

Cyrus R. Vance Center for International Justice, Earth Law Center and International Rivers (2020), 'Rights of rivers. A global survey of the rapidly developing rights of nature jurisprudence pertaining to rivers', https://3waryu2g9363hdvii1ci666p-wpengine.netdna-ssl.com/wp-content/uploads/sites/86/2020/09/Right-of-Rivers-Report-V3-Digital-compressed.pdf

ECMIA (2021) 'Aportes del enlace continental de mujeres indígenas de las Américas (ECMIA) y CHIRAPAQ Centro de culturas indígenas del Perú sobre el borrador de la recomendación general n*39 sobre los derechos de las mujeres y niñas indígenas'

Fajardo, Lennys (2021) 'No vamos a comer eucaliptos: las mujeres Qom se organizan para preservar su territorio', *Red de desarollo sostenible Honduras*, https://portal.rds.hn/archivos/4328

FAO/AECDI (2021), La protección de los derechos de las mujeres rurales en América Latina, estado actual de la legislación y políticas existentes en el contexto de post pandemia COVID-19', https://intercoonecta.aecid.es/Gestin%20del%20conocimiento/Mujeres-Rurales-%20derechos.pdf

FIMI (2021) 'Input to the committee on the draft of the CEDAW general recommendation no. 39 on the rights of indigenous women and girls, *OHCR*, https://www.ohchr.org/EN/HRBodies/CEDAW/Pages/Draft-GR-rights-Indigenous-women-and-girls.aspx

FIMI (2020) Global study on the situation of indigenous women and girls in the framework of the 25th anniversary of the Beijing declaration and platform for action, https://fimi-iiwf.org/wp-content/uploads/2020/09/GlobalStudyFIMI_20-englishRGB-2.pdf

FIMI (2006) 'Mairin Iwanka Raya. Indigenous women stand against violence. a companion report to the United Nations secretary', General Study on Violence Against Women

Hivos (2021) 'Demanding justice for indigenous peoples', https://hivos.org/news/demanding-justice-for-Indigenous-peoples

CIDH (2015) 'Pueblos indígenas, comunidades afrodescendientes y recursos naturales', http://www.oas.org/es/cidh/informes/pdfs/industriasextractivas2016.pdf

Mayara M. et al. (2018) 'Agronegocio e injusticia ambiental: los impactos sobre la salud de las mujeres del campo', *WRM*, https://wrm.org.uy/es/boletines/nro-236

Minga (2022) 'Suprema acoge recurso de protección de comunidades indígenas contra proyecto de grupo Errázuriz para explotar litio en salar de Maricunga en Atacama', *El Ciudadano*, https://www.elciudadano.com/actualidad/suprema-acoge-recurso-de-proteccion-de-comunidades-indigenas-contra-proyecto-de-grupo-errazuriz-para-explotar-litio-en-salar-de-maricunga-en-atacama/02/15/?msclkid=e584fb39a81b11ecb782c8bcc8db4a19

Morales De la Cruz, A. (2022) 'In the Ecuadorian Amazon, Wituk facepainting is an act of resistance'. *Vogue*, https://www.vogue.com/article/kichwa-women-sarayaku-amazon-wituk-face-painting

Muñoz Cabrera, P. (2018), 'Campos baldios: extrativismo e violências interseccionais', *Cadernos Adenauer* 19(1), pp.161–175, https://www.kas.de/wf/doc/25929-1442-5-30.pdf

Muñoz Cabrera, P. (2019) 'A justiça de gênero na América Latina: convergências e dissonâncias nos contextos analíticos feministas', in: Alterman Blay, E. et al. (eds.) *Gênero e feminismos: Argentina, Brasil e Chile en transformaçao.* Sao Paulo: EDUSP/FAPESP

Observatorio Ciudadano (2018) 'Ercilia Araya – el primer panel sobre las violaciones de derechos humanos de pueblos indígenas en dictadura', https://www.youtube.com/watch?v=RgyXANt8qnY

Raízes (2018) 'Povos indígenas e quilombolas: 3 motivos pelos quais a demarcação de terras é importante', *Raízes*, https://raizesds.com.br/pt/povos-indigenas-quilombolas

Solano Ortíz, L (2015) 'Mujer, violencia e industria minera', *REDULAM*, http://redulam.org/guatemala/mujer-violencia-e-industria-minera

UN (1995) 'Report of the fourth world conference on women Beijing, 4-15 September 1995', https://www.un.org/womenwatch/daw/beijing/pdf/Beijing%20full%20report%20E.pdf

UN (2010) 'Declaration for health, life and defense of our land, rights and future Generations', 1st International Indigenous Women's Environmental and Reproductive Health Symposium, June 30 – July 1, UN Permanent Forum's 10th session, https://www.un.org/esa/socdev/unpfii/documents/EGM12_carmen_waghiyi.pdf>

UN (2007) 'UNDRIP – United Nations declaration of the rights of indigenous people', https://www.un.org/development/desa/Indigenouspeoples/wp-content/uploads/sites/19/2018/11/UNDRIP_E_web.pdf

Via Campesina (2003) 'Que es la soberania alimentaria. La via campesina – movimiento campesino internacional', https://viacampesina.org/es/que-es-la-soberania-alimentaria

World Rainforest Movement (2014) 'Women and oil: the struggle for Sumak Kawsay', *WRM Bulletin* 200, 5 April, https://www.wrm.org.uy/bulletin-articles/women-and-oil-the-struggle-for-sumak-kawsay

World Rainforest Movement (2021) 'Mesoamerican meeting of communities against oil palm', *WRM Bulletin*, 17 December, https://www.wrm.org.uy/bulletin-articles/mesoamerican-meeting-of-communities-against-oil-palm

CHAPTER 5
'I have rights and I am free': Resisting gendered intersectional violence against Latin American migrant women

Cathy McIlwaine

Ana is a 51-year-old migrant woman from Bolivia living in London with insecure immigration status. She spoke of how she had suffered years of domestic abuse and was initially afraid to report to the police because of her status. With the help of a migrant organization, she was able to leave her abusive partner, access support, and regularize her status. She recounted:

> 'He mistreated me, he hurt me, and I had to think twice before telling the police. But I am not afraid anymore. I have been stepped on for too long and now I stand up for myself. I have rights and I am free.' (McIlwaine, Granada & Valenzuela-Oblitas, 2019: 2)

As migrant women cross borders, gender norms and practices change across different spheres – whether dealing with state immigration regulations or trying to secure jobs and access housing. Even the way they run households can potentially change. Their experiences of gendered and intersectional violence in both private and public spheres also vary, as they negotiate misogyny and unequal gendered power relations in environments bolstered by further gendered structural and institutional violence. Take, for example, immigration regimes that are unwelcome to migrants. The State and its institutions facilitate gendered violence and this itself can make migrant women more vulnerable to abuse, as perpetrators exploit women's insecure immigration status and the discrimination they face as migrants. This chapter addresses the multiple forms of gendered violence that migrant women from Latin America experience, and the challenges they face in securing help and support as they struggle for their rights in hostile settings defined by precarious jobs, lack of language proficiency, racism, and exclusion. Nationality, race, and class intersect especially closely for migrant women as they experience direct and indirect gendered violence, with Latin American women from Afro-descendant and Indigenous backgrounds facing more barriers than others. It is also important to note that Latin Americans migrate from their various home countries for many reasons, but especially due to poverty, armed and urban conflict, lack of economic opportunities, gender-based violence, and to be reunified with their families (McIlwaine & Bunge, 2016).

Despite this, just as Ana states, Latin American migrant women are not passive in the face of widespread institutional hostility. This chapter discusses how Latin American migrant women develop informal ways of addressing violence and exclusion together, through collective initiatives coordinated by migrants' and women's rights organizations who often provide safe havens for survivors of direct gender-based violence. These organizations, most of them led by women, offer key support for Latin Americans to navigate the formal mechanisms of support on offer, and to foster social change at an institutional and policy level. Importantly, these organizations also support migrant women in more fundamental and emotional dimensions, with arts-based and participatory approaches often leading to networks of peer support and strengthening paths of self-care and self-determination. While the chapter mentions cases from other contexts, the focus is on the experiences of Latin American migrants in London and ties in closely with the third episode of our podcast series, titled 'Step Up Migrant Women'.[1]

How do Latin American migrant women experience and respond to gendered intersectional violence?

Violence can be both a cause and a characteristic of migration, involving the movement of victims of trafficking and smuggling; cases of child, early, and forced marriage, and various forms of domestic servitude through marriage or migrant domestic service. In addition, migrant women can face multiple types of direct physical, sexual, and psychological gender-based violence across public and private spheres whether they move within Latin America or migrate beyond the continent. These are rarely one-off incidents, but part of a wider mosaic of overlapping violent experiences along a continuum. But it is next to impossible to meaningfully compare the levels of gender-based violence among migrant women to those among non-migrant women. Despite a tendency to assume that levels are higher amongst the former, there is limited empirical evidence for this and there is certainly nothing inherent about the cultures women migrate from leading to higher propensities for perpetration. Male violence against migrant women is not an individual act but is linked to wider structural and symbolic violence rooted in gendered, racial, and class power hierarchies that can place migrants in vulnerable situations. Migrant women therefore often end up experiencing complex intersectional subordination from global to local levels. This clearly plays out through exclusion and hostile immigration regimes. Despite this, even within such circuits, migrant women develop informal strategies of resistance, sometimes referred to as 'small acts' as they can appear limited to outsiders.

In the UK for example, the Latin American migrant community has steadily grown in recent years to approximately a quarter of a million people, of which 145,000 live in London. Although many are highly qualified and skilled, language barriers and a lack of understanding of the British employment system mean women are often forced into low-skilled and low-paid jobs such as cleaning. In these roles, conditions are often exploitative, with long hours and many women experiencing regular violations of labour rights, abuse, and exploitation (McIlwaine & Bunge, 2016). Migrant women's precarious situations of structural violence and exploitation provides fertile ground for abusive partners to behave with impunity. As Márcia, a 42-year-old Brazilian migrant in the UK who identifies as Black, states:

> 'Here you're on your own... he took advantage of that because he knew I had nowhere to go... I think the abusive man takes advantage of the fact that we're far away from family and friends.'

As noted above, these structural exclusions also underpin gendered labour abuses and harassment in the workplace, in public spaces, and in (state and non-state) institutions, as well as in the domestic sphere (McIlwaine & Evans, 2018: 38).

Research has shown that incidence of gender-based violence among Brazilian migrants in London is very high – at 82 per cent across their lifetime, with almost half suffering emotional/psychological violence, 38 per cent experiencing physical violence, and 14 per cent experiencing sexual violence. Almost a third of this was domestic violence (30 per cent), with a quarter perpetrated by an intimate partner.[2] A key issue related to gender-based violence among Brazilians and Latin American migrant women more widely is its sheer diversity. For example, in focus groups with 15 Brazilian women and 6 Brazilian men in London, we identified a total of 18 different types of gender-based violence. While much of this was intimate partner violence including forced detention, jealousy, defamation, stalking, femicide, and economic abuse, it also involved sexual harassment at work and on public transport (McIlwaine & Evans, 2018).

Migrant women's immigration status often generates multiple forms of direct and indirect gender-based violence and is a major source of insecurity and power inequalities individually, institutionally, and structurally. Take Estela's case for example. A 31-year-old Mexican woman, Estela migrated to London with a domestic service visa. When her employers refused to renew her visa, she felt she had no other choice but to marry her Portuguese boyfriend. Their relationship soon disintegrated through physical, verbal, and economic abuse on his part. For example, Estela spoke of how he withheld family welfare support:

> 'He was being paid housing benefit at that time and spent all the money... I had to pay all the rent and was frustrated with the fact that I had to pay all the expenses and have the baby.'

Estela also spoke of the racist attacks her boyfriend subjected her to, especially when she eventually reported him to the authorities. She noted:

> 'He tells me "How is it possible that a small and ugly Third Worlder has done this to me?" He thinks he's of the First World because he is Portuguese, me third because I come from Mexico'.

However, Estela's story is one of resilience and resourcefulness as well as violence; in the face of not being able to renew her visa, she managed to remain in the UK, subsequently leaving her abusive partner and securing help, albeit after suffering considerable distress (McIlwaine, Granada & Valenzuela-Oblitas, 2019).

Gendered intersectional violence and widespread exploitative working practices have long been afflicted on female migrant workers. The experiences of Latin American migrant domestic workers in the US in particular have received considerable attention. Reports reveal abuse from employers and states who often ignore the plight of domestic workers who may have irregular status and/or are treated as 'one of the family'. In a recent study of 516 Latin domestic workers in the Texas/Mexican border region, one-third of elder care workers had been shouted at, 20 per cent had been threatened, and 11 per cent had been pushed or physically hurt. Among house cleaners, 19 per cent had been pushed or physically hurt by their employer or another person within the employer's home. Live-in workers were the most abused with 31 per cent having been pushed or physically hurt by an employer and 45 per cent being injured on the job (National Domestic Workers Alliance, 2018:3).

Migrant workers often experience a combination of different types of gendered violence compounded by wider discrimination against migrant women who are often essentialized, 'othered', and exoticized. Such was the case of Sabrina, 44, from Brazil who was brought to

London by a Brazilian family to work as a nanny. Sabrina entered with a tourist visa and her employers confiscated her passport after she arrived; she soon became an overstayer when her visa expired. Sabrina was expected not only to work as a nanny, but also to clean and work for the family's commercial cleaning business, all for £100 per week. In addition to being imprisoned in the house, she was also sexually abused by her male boss who threatened her with a kitchen knife and said he'd report her to the authorities because she was undocumented. Thankfully, Sabrina did manage to leave with the help of some friends. She then secured another job as a cleaner and received support from a migrant organization (McIlwaine & Evans, 2018, 2022).

Among Brazilian women in London, sexualized discrimination applies regardless of their occupations and backgrounds. For example, 27-year-old Fernanda who worked as a teacher in London discussed an encounter at a professional annual schools' conference:

> 'Then one lunchtime, this new fourth grade teacher, he came up to me and said, "With those skirts you could make 200 bucks!" I told him to disappear, and I carried on with my life, but that got stuck in my throat, you can't say that to someone.' (McIlwaine & Evans, 2018: 21)

Trans women migrants often experience disproportionate levels of gendered violence because of endemic discrimination and exclusion. Nina, a trans woman from Brazil, spoke of her former job as a sex worker where she was physically and sexually abused by both her clients and her boyfriend; she also discussed how she was regularly harassed in the streets of London because she was a trans woman. However, Nina had also managed to leave sex work, secure support from a migrant women's organization, and was taking a computer course (McIlwaine, Granada & Valenzuela-Oblitas, 2019). It is important to note that Nina was also deaf; on arrival in the UK she had to learned British Sign Language (BSL) as it differed from the Brazilian version she had learned as a child. This also highlights the importance of disability as another key aspect of discrimination potentially making migrant women survivors even more vulnerable. Indeed, Nina noted that it particularly affected her ability to initially access support services.

Crossing the border itself can entail gender-based intersectional harassment. In the specific situation of dealing with immigration authorities, Camila, a Brazilian migrant from Bahia who identifies as mixed race, spoke of her experience at a London airport:

> 'After I'd been interviewed for three hours, I was released to go get my luggage. An immigration officer accompanied me into the lift to take me to where my luggage was. Inside the lift he

said, "Wow, you've got beautiful breasts. Can I touch them?" Something like that. I looked at him and thought, "I've just arrived, and the harassment has already started?" I told him no and felt afraid inside the lift. He continued to praise me and chat me up, but I was shocked, not understanding how something like this could happen in such a formal place, inside immigration.' (McIlwaine & Evans, 2018: 20)

This has also been discussed within Latin America in a study with Venezuelan and Colombian migrants who travelled 4,500 kms from Cali in Colombia to Antofagasta in Chile. They faced explicit sexist and racist abuse on the part of border officials, the police, and other borderland actors who often arbitrarily refused them entry. In one instance, a Chilean border official insinuated that an Afro-Colombian woman was entering with the intention of engaging in sex work. Yet again, women spoke of exercising some limited agency along their journeys. While it was not an overt form of resistance as such, women spoke of having to '*aguantar*' (endure/cope) as a type of defiance to the hardships they faced (Ryburn, 2021).[3]

Therefore, the migration process is inherently violent, and violence – including gender-based, urban, and armed – is often a major driver of migration in the first place (McIlwaine, 2014). However, moving is a form of exercising agency, albeit constrained and invariably in the context of precarity. Many women in the Latin American community in London have experienced gender-based violence in their home countries at various times throughout the course of their lives. Among Brazilian women, for example, 77 per cent reported experiences of gender-based violence prior to moving to London, of which a third was perpetrated by intimate partners and other family members (McIlwaine & Evans, 2018). Some Latin American women stated explicitly that they moved in order to flee gender-based violence. Natalia, a 49-year-old Ecuadorian woman, spoke of how she left because of spousal abuse:

'I was a craft teacher in the Catholic Church in the Ecuadorian Episcopal Congregation. I didn't move for economic reasons, but because my husband was treating me really badly – physically and mentally, I needed to leave, so I decided to flee for Europe.' (McIlwaine & Bunge, 2016).

Others migrated with abusive partners in an effort to improve their difficult relationships, only for them to deteriorate on arrival as the wider structural and symbolic violence of living as a migrant put pressure on them. This was the case for 37-year-old Cristina from Brazil who identifies as mixed race. Cristina moved to London in a bid to

---

Box 5.1: From undocumented to homeless to campaigner: the case of Gilmara

In 2016, Gil, as everyone calls her, experienced the nightmare of British institutions' hostility towards migrants. It started when she migrated from Brazil to the UK with a British partner, first entering as a tourist, under the premise that they'd sort out her visa after arrival. She arrived with her nine-year-old son from a previous relationship and her and her partner's younger child. Gil's controlling partner actively allowed her original visa to expire, leaving her undocumented. This caused the abuse to intensify, as her partner threatened to report her either to the police or immigration authorities and threatened to take custody of her children. In addition, Gil was further hindered by the fact that she wasn't familiar with the law in the UK and was still learning English.

Despite these barriers, Gil eventually found the courage to seek help, running away from her home and going straight to the police station with her eldest daughter. In her own words, Gil narrates the institutional violence she faced through her interactions with British institutions because she had No Recourse to Public Funds (NRPF), in our Women Resisting Violence podcast:

'I stayed on the street to get help, went to the police and tried to explain everything in English, which is very difficult... My experience was of real hostility, the police saying they weren't a hotel and I should seek help in my embassy or in immigration to return to my country, though at that point I had fled from this man who, as perpetrator, remained with the custody of our child. I thought I'd be listened to and given shelter but I was not... When I went to the Home Office to ask for a voluntary return, I said to myself I couldn't stay on the streets, I had my family in Brazil, my mum's house, so I said please, send me back there, I have my documents here, ticket and so on. But at the home office, they're not prepared for you asking to go back... They were not prepared to give me support and said, "unfortunately there's nothing we can do. Do you have somewhere to go? Do you know anyone here?" The only person I knew was the perpetrator. So, I ended up going to a different police department, staying there until someone could get me into a hostel.'

Processing everything, she explains that 'When we go for help, we generate more questions about who we are and about our status rather than concern about our safety... the process was of leaving an abusive relationship and [I ended up] finding myself suddenly homeless'.

Gil has since become an activist, campaigning for changes in legal protections to migrant survivors of domestic violence in the UK. She's also become a support worker in a peer support group with the Latin American Women's Rights Service. Gil shares her story nowadays as an agent for change. In 2020, four years after her experience, she spoke in Parliament as a witness in a Public Bill Committee on the Domestic Abuse Bill. Now working to support other women living through similar struggles, Gil speaks of her sense of a mission: 'I work with women today, I explain to them that they each have their own story but they are not alone, that I have already been through the same thing.'

Sources: Women Resisting Violence podcast episode 3: Step Up Migrant Women, Domestic Abuse Bill Deb, 4 June 2020, c25.

save her marriage, but the violence worsened in the UK as her husband strangled her, threatened her with knives, and tried to sexually assault her (McIlwaine & Evans, 2020) (see also Box 5.1).

Gendered intersectional violence and the hostile immigration environment

Although migrant women's experiences are differentiated by class, race, nationality, sexuality, and other identities, their immigration status is central to understanding their exposure to gender-based violence. Undocumented migrant women or those under temporary visas are susceptible to various forms of exploitation which, in turn, become precipitating factors to further engender violence against them. Yet this must be situated within the context of 'hostile immigration environments', which are not specific to the UK. Immigration legislation and judicial and welfare support services actively create intimidating and unaccommodating environments for migrants. In the UK, migrants' rights have been systematically eroded for decades and most acutely since 2010, with the Immigration Acts of 2014 and 2016 entailing ever more severe enforcement of immigration controls by hospitals, banks, public sector organizations, private landlords, and others. A key aspect of this has been the No Recourse to Public Funds (NRPF) restriction attached to many temporary visas (visitor, spouse, student, or tourist) preventing access to state benefits, housing, or other statutory assistance including publicly subsidized refuges and the criminal justice system. Despite some concessions for women who are destitute and/or there are safeguarding issues around children, most women are excluded.[4]

In this environment, immigration enforcement is prioritized over migrant women's human rights. This means that a lack of safe reporting mechanisms prevents migrant women from fleeing gender-based violence, with many staying with perpetrators because they have no alternative (see Box 5.2 below). Migrant women are afraid to report their experiences of gender-based violence to the police and other statutory services because they risk their data being shared with the immigration control authorities. In recent research with over 70 migrant women in London (including Latin Americans), 62 per cent stated that their perpetrator had threatened their deportation if she reported the abuses, with another 62 per cent feeling they would not be supported due to their immigration status, revealing a widespread distrust of the police and public authorities. Manipulation through immigration status was a widespread issue reported by many women from a range of nationalities. For example, 43-year-old Marisol from Colombia noted:

'My partner threatened me with calling the Home Office, saying that the Home Office will deport me back to my country. I felt nervous, all day with depression, I felt desperate if he called the Home Office, even if he didn't call, because I would be deported. I think profoundly that he wouldn't do it but still I felt fear and anxiety. I had to stay with him because I think that I depend on him. He has threatened my family and has been verbally abusive in the UK... I have a temporary visa of two and a half years I have been refused spousal visas several times, so was undocumented for six years. I was very vulnerable.' (McIlwaine, Granada & Valenzuela-Oblitas, 2019: 16–17)

These types of situations are compounded by language barriers, fear of losing custody of children, and of losing a home and/or income. While interactions with the police are not uniformly negative, they tend to be characterized by favouring perpetrators over victims/ survivors, regardless of women's immigration status. For example, Maria, a 32-year-old migrant from Brazil, revealed how while pregnant with twins, she had defended herself from a knife attack by her former partner who had subsequently called the police. On arrival at their home, the police arrested Maria and took her to the police station because her partner had blamed the incident on her because he could speak English and she could not. She then spent three hours clarifying the situation with the help of a translator and recalled:

'I thought the world had ended, you know? Why was I being arrested, why was I inside a cell if I hadn't done anything wrong?'

Maria was one of many Brazilian women who stated that the police had widespread discretionary powers (McIlwaine & Evans, 2018). Gil, also Brazilian, speaks of her similar experiences in our Women Resisting Violence podcast (see also Box 5.1).

Far from improving, this environment is seen to be becoming ever more inhabitable over time, as Elizabeth Jiménez-Yáñez, Policy and Communications Coordinator at the Latin American Women's Rights Services (LAWRS) and coordinator of the Step Up Migrant Women Campaign in the UK, speaking in our Women Resisting Violence podcast, explains:

'For instance, there has been a reduction in translation services in several state services which we saw happen from the very beginning of the pandemic. This obviously prevents women – Latin American women in this specific case – from having justice. They face barriers to reporting crimes to police because there are no translators. Police will ask you to bring your son as a translator. So obviously there is a system lacking in ethics and a danger of revictimization'.

This hostile immigration environment therefore allows perpetrators to weaponize immigration as a tool of power and control, leaving women with insecure status afraid of reporting to the police or social services for fear of being deported. It creates a form of gendered infrastructural violence (McIlwaine & Evans 2022). This leaves women isolated, unable to communicate and unsupported, as Elizabeth Jiménez-Yáñez (LAWRS) further explains:

> 'Another thing that happens in Latin American communities is that isolation becomes part of the abuse... Many of these women migrate alone, or exclusively with their partners, and do not have support in a country like England where the language barrier can play a principal role.'

(See also Boxes 5.1 and 5.2).

Organizations providing refuge and campaigning for change

As much of the gendered intersectional violence against migrant women is rooted in state and institutional violence, it is no surprise that state services dedicated to aiding women survivors of gendered violence often fail migrant women seeking help. In the face of widespread institutional hostility and embodied fears, migrants' and women's rights organizations often provide safe havens for survivors of gender-based violence, complementing the informal initiatives developed by women migrants to address the violence they have experienced.

These organizations offer key support for migrant women in a range of specialist areas, including legal advice, psychological assistance, language translation, and childcare provision to help survivors deal with their experiences of intersecting direct and structural violence and their long-term traumatic effects. They also manage to form key channels of communication with the formal mechanisms of support, including with referrals, which makes them active members of the broader infrastructures of support to migrant women. What's more, these organizations, most of them led by migrant women, are also active in accompanying women survivors through the more formal mechanisms, alleviating and often preventing the negative experiences of gendered infrastructural violence in police stations, health units, and the justice system. Organizations such as the LAWRS in London have provided support for Latin American women in various guises since 1983.[5] Their support has provided lifelines for many women such as Gil (see Box 5.1), as well as for women such as Miriam, 46, from Brazil:

> 'They gave me guidance and supported me from the beginning to the end, through two and a half years of court hearings... I won my case, thankfully, with the support of LAWRS... as I don't speak English very well, I had the help of a lot of volunteer interpreters.' (McIlwaine & Evans, 2018: 31)

Not only have they helped individual women, but LAWRS has also fostered collective engagements among women, such as mutual support groups and women's collectives with the aim of building confidence and healing. For example, they created a group called Sin Fronteras (No Limits) to work with young Latin American women aged 14-21 on preventing violence. This is a mutual support network that develops participatory activities using creative and performance arts, with a focus on developing self-esteem, rights education, and empowerment. The case of Sin Fronteras also highlights the importance of age as a key aspect of migrant women's intersectional experiences of gendered violence. For example, Melissa Munz, the Young Women's Project Coordinator at Sin Fronteras, spoke of the types of violence experienced by young women in London:

> 'Many of the girls live with violence at home as their mothers are survivors of domestic violence, but what they talk about most is street violence, especially those who work at night. They talk about how uncomfortable they feel travelling home, harassment situations, and the strategies they adopt to feel safer... At work they experience labour exploitation as their bosses take advantage of them because they are young. They also experience hate crimes and racism from their peers in school. Some girls talk about bias and stereotypes by state services they have approached for help or advice.' (Melissa Munz, 2022)

Yet these young women are defiant in the face of such violence. In relation to street violence, for example, some wear male clothes and talk among themselves on how to protect each other. As Melissa further notes:

> 'They are resilient and stand together for the rights of all women and girls. For them, sorority, each other's support, and dialogue are forms of resistance to those different types of violence. They are creative and they are activists. They believe that activism takes shape in many forms, and that small acts that promote equality in our daily lives are a way to contribute to social change.'

In particular, the young women are very interested in *artivism* activities (see Chapter 6) and have produced posters and videos that reflect their experiences as young migrants. Some of the Sin Fronteras participants have been involved in producing a documentary where they explore and discuss matters affecting their lives like migration, age discrimination, and community spaces in London.[6]

Another example is the feminist collective Women Activist Revolutionary Migrant Intersectional (WARMI), which was developed from LAWRS's community activist project in which Latin American migrant women wielded their lived experiences as a tool for their social transformation. Maria, a WARMI member states: 'Warmi is a Quechua word that means a powerful woman who loves her family, a brave warrior, and for us it means fighting, respect, and solidarity, being united'. Similar examples of migrant organizations providing essential support for Latin American migrant women abound within and beyond Latin America. In London, organizations such as Latin American Women's Aid (LAWA) and the Indoamerican Refugee and Migrant Organization (IRMO) provide core services for women. In Latin America, one of the largest and most dangerous migration routes in the continent entails movement from Central America (often from Honduras, El Salvador and Guatemala, and often fleeing endemic urban violence) through Mexico, as migrants try to reach the US. A range of organizations on this route provide support and services for women migrants, especially those who have experienced gender-based violence in their home countries or on their journeys. These include the Instituto para las Mujeres en la Migración (IMUMI) which promotes migrant women's rights in Mexico.

Box 5.2: Resistance through advocacy: Step Up Migrant Women campaign

The Step Up Migrant Women campaign was established by LAWRS in 2017 and is led 'by and for' migrant women. It has entailed the creation of a coalition of over 50 organizations (currently 57) from the human rights, migrant, and women's rights sectors to advocate for support for migrant women who are prevented from accessing safe support, healthcare, and refuge when escaping gender-based violence. Focusing specifically on migrant women with an insecure immigration status, the campaign fights for safe reporting mechanisms in the UK and highlights the precedence of immigration control over human rights, as well as the lack of specific guidelines on how police officers should deal with migrant victims of gender-based violence.

Step Up Migrant Women was especially active during the preparation and passing of the UK's Domestic Abuse Act 2021, drawing attention to how immigration laws add to women's vulnerability to gender-based violence. They lobbied to ensure that migrant women with insecure status were included in support mechanisms, being partially successful with two amendments being passed concerning victims' personal data for immigration purposes. However, many other propositions were rejected by the committee, failing to challenge the highly complex and harmful conditions under which migrant women experience gender-based violence in the UK.

In our Women Resisting Violence podcast, Elizabeth Jiménez-Yáñez, the coordinator of the campaign spoke of the collaborative process of documenting and sharing stories to influence this legislative process:

'From the start of this legislative process, LAWRS and Step Up, together with organizations, got involved to seek specific changes in the bill... We collected information, collected case studies, and came with all this wealth of information provided by the organizations and shared it with decision makers... showing collectively that barriers that migrant women face are not isolated but structural'.

Elizabeth laments: 'Our position is that sadly – despite some concessions made in terms of safe reporting and a pilot project to offer accommodation to migrant women – the law does not respond to the need and urgency of protecting migrant women.'

Step Up Migrant Women has also conducted research in order to provide evidence from which to lobby. This resulted in the report *The Right to be Believed*, based on a survey and interviews with over 70 migrant women from 22 different countries, many of them Latin American. The report highlights the importance of ethical engagements between researchers and migrant organizations, where migrant women survivors are themselves the experts whose views must shape campaigns and policy prescriptions in order to reflect their needs and demands.

Sources: McIlwaine (2021b), Jiménez-Yáñez & McIlwaine (2021), McIlwaine, Granada & Valenzuela-Oblitas (2019)

As well as providing a culturally sensitive and non-judgemental support community, organizations such as LAWRS also work to promote social change at advocacy and policy levels. They have done this most prominently and most successfully through their Step Up Migrant Women campaign established by LAWRS in 2017 and discussed by Elizabeth Jiménez-Yáñez on our Women Resisting Violence podcast (see Box 5.2).

Latin American migrant women resisting gendered intersectional violence through the arts

Success stories where migrant women have managed to break away from violent relationships are often noted by service providers, highlighting how their intervention can be crucial to set women on the right track towards accessing essential statutory services and the criminal justice system. But perhaps less acknowledged is that organizations also support migrant women in more affective dimensions, often leading to networks of peer support and strengthening paths of self-care and self-determination. As indicated above in relation to the cases of Sin Fronteras and WARMI, Latin American migrant women have been at the forefront of developing artistic initiatives as therapy among survivors of gendered violence. In addition, Latin American artists have also played a role in raising awareness and highlighting the plight of survivors, especially in light of the continuing taboo around many aspects of gendered intersectional violence.

One example of the latter is the recent work by Brazilian theatre- and filmmaker, Gaël Le Cornec, who I collaborated with on creating the verbatim theatre play, *Efêmera,* which was based on research on gender-based violence with Brazilian migrant women in London (McIlwaine & Evans, 2018). *Efêmera* was not a participatory or therapeutic initiative, but rather reflects Gaël's interpretations of Brazilian migrant women's lives in London developed into a dramatic narrative to highlight their experiences, raise awareness, and to break taboos. Indeed, in light of the need to share the story of *Efêmera* beyond the theatre, a video was made titled 'Raising Awareness of Violence Against Brazilian Women and Girls in London'.[7] This was further supplemented by the creation of a short film, *Ana,* as a short version of *Efêmera,* which was screened at the Davis Feminist Film Festival in the US; Vox Feminae Festival in Croatia; Wow Festival in Jordan, Morocco, and Tunisia; the Kautik Festival in India; and was a finalist at the NYC Directed by Women festival in the US.[8] Gaël notes that these activities are all forms of activism: 'Activism has the power to change the future, right?... For me as an artist, my work is always about creating awareness. Art can pressure to make change happen and support the change.' (See Box 5.3).

Box 5.3: Resistance through theatre: *Efêmera* by Gaël Le Cornec

Efêmera was a verbatim theatre play written by Gaël Le Cornec, based on research on gender-based violence against Brazilian migrant women in London led by Cathy McIlwaine. First performed at the Southwark Playhouse in London 2017, there were also performances in Rio de Janeiro (Centro de Artes de Maré and Sede das Cias, see Figure 5.1) in 2017 and the Warren Theatre in Brighton, England in 2018.

The play developed a portrayal of Ana (played by Gaël Le Cornec) who retold her experiences of gendered violence back home in Brazil and in the UK to Joanne, a British documentary filmmaker (played by Rosie Macpherson). Ana's story reflected on multiple incidences of intimate partner and wider institutional urban violence experienced by many of the women interviewed. These were played out on stage through physical re-enactments of fights between Ana and Joanne. Such artistic interpretations are deeply embodied and can provide visceral interpretations and insight into how gendered insecurity and fear is so deeply embedded in women's lives across borders.

Gaël reflects on the creation of the play:

'I basically started analysing it [the research], but in artistic ways, and trying to understand what these women were going through, what were the main issues they were facing, what were the patterns of violence that kept coming back... That character [Ana] was an amalgamation of all the women interviewed... but what I wanted to do with *Efêmera* was to push boundaries of what a verbatim play could be. I wanted to see if I could somehow shift between the real and fictional realms.'

The responses from the audience to *Efêmera* in Brighton highlight the transnationality of experiences of a migrant woman living in the UK from another country: 'It spoke to me on a personal and deep level. As a Mexican-American who has been sexually abused as a child and later on helped others deal with the same issues'. Yet, it also resonated with women who had less in common with the protagonist's story: 'As a middle-class white English woman who has been sexually assaulted/raped even – the stories were close to my heart'.

Sources: Stevens, Le Cornec & McIlwaine (2021); McIlwaine (2021a)

Figure 5.1: Theatre poster for *Efêmera* in Rio de Janeiro, 2017

Another example of working with the arts to address and resist gender-based violence is a theatre project discussed in our Women Resisting Violence podcast. The *Lutamos No Escuro* or *We Still Fight in the Dark* project[9] is based on the same research and is developed by Migrants in Action (MinA) and led by Carolina Cal Angrisani. Carolina established the organization MinA in 2018 as a community theatre group advocating for the wellbeing and visibility of the Brazilian community in the UK and Europe. The project is based on the report *We can't fight in the dark* (McIlwaine and Evans, 2018) and entails a reinterpretation of the research findings through eight creative applied arts workshops designed to improve wellbeing, develop community healing, and raise the visibility of gender-based violence through an artistic installation/video. The workshops were held both online and in person between 2021 and 2022 and combined theatre, music, writing, and poetry workshops, together with in-person gatherings, to create the final film installation (see Figure 5.2). When the women were asked about their expectations of participating in the project in the first workshop, one woman noted how she wanted to:

Figure 5.2: Poem by a MinA workshop participant during the *We Still Fight in the Dark* project

'Take away from me the hurt from two whole years, using the arts, my own body expression; take away from my body everything that does not belong to me. Everything that comes from others and that I have been carrying like a heavy suitcase full of clothes that no longer fit me.'

The participants were overwhelmingly positive about their experiences at the end of the process:

'The project... has been amazing, not only to strengthen connections with people I already knew but also to bond with other women, listen to their stories, their pains and victories and celebrate that this is not an easy life as an immigrant alongside Brazilian women so diverse and at the same time very similar in their challenges and struggles.'

Through arts-based and participatory approaches, organizations can offer long-term and tailored support to build bonds between women from diverse backgrounds sharing their struggles as migrants away from home. Through these initiatives, women co-create means of actively resisting gender-based violence collectively, actively changing the course of their own lives.

It is worth noting that the work with MinA was all conducted during the COVID-19 pandemic. This is especially important given that it is widely acknowledged that migrant women everywhere have disproportionately suffered from domestic violence during COVID lockdowns. It has been argued that hostile immigration regimes (see above) mean that women with insecure immigration status and No Recourse to Public Funds have faced intensified barriers to safe reporting and obtaining support. During the pandemic, migrant women have been even more fearful than before of reporting abuse for risk of detention and deportation. In addition, the pandemic has pushed many migrant women further into poverty as they have lost their jobs, with support from migrant organizations being cut back as they struggle to secure sustainable financial support[10] (McIlwaine, 2020)

Conclusion

This chapter has examined the ways in which Latin American migrant women experience direct gender-based violence and the ways in which this intersects with racialized state and institutional violence, especially when they have insecure immigration status. Minoritized migrant women are not automatically vulnerable to gendered violence because of the cultures from where they come, but due to exploitation and manipulation by multiple individual and state perpetrators within the context of hostile immigration regimes in the UK and beyond. However, the discussion has also noted how women are not passive victims of violence, but rather resist in informal and formal ways. While reporting to the judicial and other state authorities can be fraught with dangers for migrant women, migrant and women's organizations provide much-needed culturally sensitive support. These organizations not only provide support services for women to challenge and resist intersectional gender-based violence, but also engage in campaigning and advocacy work, such as the Step Up Migrant Women campaign. Others use the arts to raise awareness and work directly with minoritized migrant women survivors to find ways to resist and develop mechanisms of self-care and solidarity.

Notes

1. This chapter draws on research collaborations through three projects directed by McIlwaine: Transnational VAWG https://transnationalviolenceagainstwomen.org/the-researches/transnational-vawg, We Still Fight in the Dark https://transnationalviolenceagainstwomen.org/the-researches/research-projects-we-still-fight-in-the-dark and Step Up Migrant Women https://cathymcilwaine.info/research-projects/step-up-migrant-women. The first is funded by the ESRC (ES/N013247/1), the second by the ESRC Impact Acceleration Account (IAA) held at King's College London, and the third by the Latin American Women's Rights Service and the Lloyd's Foundation.
2. This research draws on engagements with Brazilian migrants in London involving a quantitative survey with 175 women, together with 25 in-depth interviews and 5 focus group discussions, as well as service mapping of organizations providing support for women victims-survivors of violence based on interviews with representatives from 12 providers.
3. This is shown in the video 'Navigating Borderlands', created as part of Megan Ryburn's research project Navigating Borderlands: Colombian migrant women in Chile and experiences of violence. https://youtu.be/_wb2U2TKbAE.
4. A person will have no recourse to public funds when they are 'subject to immigration control', as defined at section 115 of the Immigration and Asylum Act 1999. A person who is subject to immigration control cannot claim public funds (benefits and housing assistance) unless an exception applies. See full details at   https://www.nrpfnetwork.org.uk/information-and-resources/rights-and-entitlements/immigration-status-and-entitlements/who-has-no-recourse-to-public-funds-nrpf.
5. See Marilyn Thomson (2021) Organisations | LAWRS: https://lab.org.uk/wrv-organisations-lawrs.

6. The video 'is a celebration of our diversity, identities and cultures; a wake-up call for decision makers to act; and an invitation to other youth groups, feminists, and minority communities to join forces and support us in our role as agents of change in the British society.' Watch *This is who we are: Sin Fronteras* at https://youtu.be/HGPNE1bULnw.

7. This inter-disciplinary project documented the experiences of women survivors of VAWG through surveys, testimonial interviews, and focus group discussions as well as using a range of artistic practices through verbatim theatre, film, and audio-visual installation work to highlight the importance and impact of this phenomenon. It shows not only alarmingly high rates of incidence but also the deep-seated negative effects of VAWG on women's wellbeing. The video, directed by Aida Baneres, with animation by Francesca da Bassa and music from Cesc Fonoll, is available to watch on YouTube: https://youtu.be/LPDNxtWB9e0.

8. For more information on *Efêmera*, see https://gaellecornec1.wixsite.com/efemera. For more information on *Ana*, see https://www.footprintproductions.co.uk/film-ana.

9. This project is a collaboration between MinA, Cathy McIlwaine and Niall Sreenan (from the Policy Institute at King's), Renata Peppl (People's Palace Projects) and with support from LAWRS. See also Organisations/Migrants in Action: https://lab.org.uk/wrv-organisations-migrants-in-action-mina.

10. See also 'Migrant Women: Failed by the State, Locked in Abuse' from the Step Up Migrant Women Campaign. Available at https://stepupmigrantwomen.org/2020/06/26/migrant-women-failed-by-the-state-locked-in-abuse.

Bibliography

Domestic Abuse Bill Deb (2020), c25, 4 June, https://www.theyworkforyou.com/pbc/2019-21/Domestic_Abuse_Bill/02-0_2020-06-04a.25.4

Jiménez-Yáñez, E. and McIlwaine, C. (2021) 'Charity researcher collaborations are key to ending gender-based violence', *Latin America Bureau*, 9 December, https://lab.org.uk/wrv-charitiy-research-advocacy

Women Resisting Violence (2021) 'Step up migrant women', https://lab.org.uk/wrv/podcast

McIlwaine, C. (2014) 'Everyday urban violence and transnational displacement of Colombian urban migrants to London', *Environment and Urbanization* 26(2), pp. 417–426, https://journals.sagepub.com/doi/full/10.1177/0956247814544416

McIlwaine, C. (2019) 'Latin Americans in the UK: an increasingly visible population', *SLAS*, https://www.slas.org.uk/post/latin-americans-in-the-uk-an-increasingly-visible-population

McIlwaine, C. (2020) 'Living in fear during the COVID-19 crisis: migrant women with insecure immigration status and domestic violence', *KCL,* https://www.kcl.ac.uk/living-in-fear-during-the-covid-19-crisis-migrant-women-with-insecure-immigration-status-and-domestic-violence

McIlwaine, C. (2021a) 'Memories of violence against women and girls across borders', in: Boesten, J. and Scanlon, H. (eds.) *Gender and memorial arts.* London: Routledge, pp. 211–229, https://kclpure.kcl.ac.uk/portal/en/publications/memories-of-violence-against-women-and-girls-across-borders(646d03c7-e425-4e48-95aa-2c59e18496f0).html

McIlwaine, C (2021b) 'Organisations | LAWRS | Step up migrant women campaign', *Latin America Bureau,* 15 September, https://lab.org.uk/wrv-organisations-lawrs-step-up-migrant-women-campaign

McIlwaine, C. and Bunge, D. (2016) 'Towards visibility: the Latin American community in London' https://kclpure.kcl.ac.uk/portal/files/107149344/Towards_Visibility_full_report.pdf

McIlwaine, C. and Evans, Y. (2018) 'We can't fight in the dark: violence against women and girls (vawg) among Brazilians in London', https://transnationalperspectivesonvawg.files.wordpress.com/2018/03/1_mcilwaine-and-evans-londonvawg-full-report_online.pdf

McIlwaine, C. and Evans, Y. (2020) 'Urban Violence Against Women and Girls (VAWG) in transnational perspective: reflections from Brazilian women in London', *International Development Planning Review* 42(1), pp. 93–112, https://kclpure.kcl.ac.uk/portal/files/101707304/Urban_Violence_Against_Women_MCLLWAINE_Accepted31August2018_GREEN_AAM.pdf

McIlwaine, C. and Evans, E. (2022) 'Navigating migrant infrastructure and gendered infrastructural violence: reflections from Brazilian women in London', *Gender, Place and Culture,* https://doi.org/10.1080/0966369X.2022.2073335

McIlwaine, C., Granada, L. and Valenzuela-Oblitas, I. (2019) 'The right to be believed', LAWRS https://kclpure.kcl.ac.uk/portal/files/110500935/The_right_to_be_believed_Full_report_final.pdf

Munz, M. (2022), interview with Marilyn Thomson, 6 May, London (email correspondence).

National Domestic Workers Alliance (2018) *Living in the shadows: Latina domestic workers in the Texas-Mexico border region.* New York: National Domestic Workers Alliance, https://actionnetwork.org/user_files/user_files/000/024/054/original/Living_in_the_Shadows_rpt_Eng_final_screen_(1)_(1).pdf

Ryburn, M. (2021) 'I don't want you in my country: migrants navigating borderland violences between Colombia and Chile', *Annals of the American Association of Geographers,* pp. 1–17, http://eprints.lse.ac.uk/112741/1/Ryburn_migrants_navigating_borderland_violences_published.pdf

Stevens, S., Le Cornec, G. and McIlwaine, C. (2021) 'What is activist art? Sophie Stevens interviews Gaël Le Cornec and Cathy McIlwaine', in: de Madeiros, A. and Kelly, D. (eds.) *Language debates: theory and reality in language learning, teaching and research.* London: John Murray Press

CHAPTER 6

'They cannot erase our memory': Commemoration, violence, and the arts

Jelke Boesten and Louise Morris

In a sprawling cemetery on the outskirts of Guatemala City, Vianney Hernández, a petite woman with a careworn face weaves her way determinedly to a grave. It has taken her hours to get there, paying for bus fares she can seldom afford. She kneels and makes a promise to her daughter, Ashly Angelie Rodriguez Hernández, buried there aged just 14: 'You... you... my girl, you know me well and I won't ever stop demanding justice for you'.

In the early hours of 8 March 2017, Ashly was burned alive, together with 40 other girls at the so-called 'Hogar Seguro' (Safe Home) Virgen de la Asunción just outside of Guatemala City. 15 more girls survived but with physical and psychological scars they will carry with them for life. The 56 girls aged between 14-17 were imprisoned by police officers in a classroom of 23 by 23 feet, with no food or sanitation, after they attempted to run away from Hogar Seguro when long-standing complaints of abuse and sexual trafficking had been ignored. A fire was started and dramatically escalated, with the girls screaming to be let out. The police officers guarding the classroom ran to alert their boss, Lucinda Maroquín, who had the key, and they reported that she said: 'Let them burn, let them burn, those dirty little bitches'. It took nine minutes for them to unlock the door. Vianney Hernández tells of the horrors of the events and the aftermath, and the families' struggles to see justice for their children, in the Women Resisting Violence podcast (Episode One: *Mourning the 56 in Guatemala*).

It seems sinisterly ironic that this massacre at a state-run children's institution took place on 8 March – International Women's Day - a sharp reminder of the brutal disregard of female life in Guatemala. While it is difficult to know the exact numbers, Guatemala is amongst the countries with the highest rates of femicide in the world, alongside El Salvador, Honduras, and Bolivia. In 2021, 531 women were murdered in Guatemala according to the *Women's Observatory*; that is 44 per month.[1] Faced with such high rates of violence against women, and such limited state intervention, it is women's groups that mobilize to resist and protest the violence they are subjected to every day.

In cases of militarized violence, for example during conflict, or institutional violence as in the case of the Guatemalan Hogar Seguro, women's resistance is not only essential, but also difficult and often dangerous. Nevertheless, up against the power of the state, it is often ordinary women who rally together, collectively seeking to honour victims, to support their families, and to demand justice through the courts, protests, and memorials. The latter public-facing demands for justice are often presented creatively: women have used symbols – like the white headscarves worn by the Mothers of the Plaza de Mayo in Argentina protesting their disappeared children, or the green kerchiefs worn at pro-abortion protests throughout Latin America. They have used performance art – as in the 'Red Carpet' protests in Peru, in which women dress in red and lie on the streets to form a carpet in protest against impunity for the violation of reproductive rights. And women have staged memorials – like the pink crosses placed in front of Court buildings to protest against femicide and impunity in Mexico, or the murals painted on Honduran and Mexican city walls to commemorate victims of femicide.[2]

Commemorative practices are essential in shaping political cultures of inclusion and in resisting impunity. Acts of violence themselves are often commemorated and publicly repudiated, providing political and social commentary on what is acceptable and what not. Acts of violence that are not remembered, are ignored, or forgotten, or even deliberately obscured and erased by complicit powers, send a message to society that gendered acts of violence are not relevant. The victims of such violence are thus not considered relevant either, not in need of protection, or justice, or prevention. Political elites benefit from the invisibility of the victims of these multiple forms of violence and silencing them perpetuates the persistence of violence and marginalization. But women consciously and unconsciously resist such erasure, which we will discuss below. This chapter will focus on women's creative acts of memorialization and commemoration and how these acts of mourning become sites of mobilization, active resistance, and empowerment (see also Boesten & Scanlon, 2021).

Political violence and gendered memory

Remembering gives us tools to analyse the present and hold history to account. For example, public acts of remembrance can help us to identify historical colonial structures in our present time and mobilize us to contribute to a more equitable, decolonial future (Lugones, 2010). Looking back on atrocities committed against particular groups of people such as women, Indigenous people, or LGBTQ+ people also allows us to frame such violence as *violence*, instead of as collateral damage or incidental occurrences. This was consolidated, for example, by women who actively and publicly protested against political violence in the 1970s, in particular in the Southern Cone.

The Mothers of the Plaza de Mayo in Argentina understood very well that their children were not only being killed by the state, but deliberately being erased from memory. They understood that this erasure gave the military dictatorship (1976-83) the possibility to continue its murderous practices. Drawing some protection from their status as mothers in a highly patriarchal society, the women of Plaza de Mayo staged the most forceful and visible protest possible during and after the years of repression, stoically circling the Plaza every Thursday armed with white headscarves and photos of their disappeared loved ones. Their protests have not been in vain: children taken from prisoners have been identified and matched up with their *abuelas*, laws have been passed, and some justice has been achieved.

Peruvian mothers did something similar in the 1980s, when their children and husbands started to disappear due to the conflict between the violent insurgent group Sendero Luminoso (Shining Path) and the Armed Forces. They first organized clandestine networks to share information and support each other's families. Then, like the Argentine mothers, they began to march with images of their loved ones, asking for justice. During the transition to democracy, after the year 2000, they stepped up their commemorative activities and became vocal activists for post-conflict justice, with demands for investigations and exhumations, and the clear marking and memorialization of burial sites. Marking the sites of the mass atrocities perpetrated by the Peruvian military is still a politically contentious issue: investigations carried out since the Truth and Reconciliation Commission was established in 2001 have recovered the remains of hundreds of people at fields behind a military base in highland Ayacucho, as well as the foundations of an oven that served to burn human remains in the 1980s. Since 2007, veterans have invaded this land to build houses, denying any relevance to what occurred in the space, or to those suffering loss after the tragic events. The mothers' organization, known as ANFASEP (Asociación Nacional de Familiares de Secuestrados Detenidos y Desaparecidos del Perú - National Association of Family Members of the Kidnapped and Disappeared in Peru), continues the fight to turn the field, La Hoyada, into a memorial site to mourn and commemorate their loved ones. Such mourning is highly political, as it not only involves commemorating the dead, but also highlighting state atrocity and impunity.

The mothers of the Plaza de Mayo and the Peruvian mothers of the disappeared of ANFASEP are responding to state violence committed during military dictatorships and political conflict. Their memorial activism is related to and can be analysed as part of what we call transitional justice - the political process that marks the transition from state violence to democracy (Boesten, 2021). Transitional justice processes generally include memorial activities, from truth-seeking processes to memory museums. Nevertheless, as recently published research in multiple transitional countries has pointed out (Boesten & Scanlon, 2021), women's representations in such memory works is often limited and grounded in stereotypes of victimhood. Beth Goldblatt and Sheila Meintjes pointed out in 1997 that the South African Truth and Reconciliation Commission (TRC) did not ask women about *their* experiences; they were expected to speak about the fate of their husbands and children. Women's own roles and contributions to the struggle, or their victimization, were downplayed or even silenced. Their roles were defined through their relationships with men and children. Of course, such conclusions help explain why the mothers of the disappeared in Argentina and Peru were considered relatively 'safe' as political actors developing motherhood and caring activities: so long as women define themselves in relation to men and children, they are not considered political actors in their own right. The activism of these mothers and wives is anything but innocent, of course. They know that their demands are political and that their memorial acts contribute to resistance and justice.

The exclusion of women's voices in much official commemorative work - TRCs, memory museums, naming practices of public spaces to commemorate heroes of war - pushes women into activism in order

---

Box 6.1: The Sepur Zarco case: sexual slavery on trial

In 2016, a groundbreaking trial took place in Guatemala, the first of its kind in Latin America. After two weeks in Guatemala's High Risk Court – which was set up especially to deal with high-profile cases requiring extra security measures due to the levels of violence and intimidation that persist within the state – two ex-military officers were convicted of sexual and domestic slavery.

The case is known as Sepur Zarco, after the community where the atrocious events took place in the 1980s during the Internal Armed Conflict. During the war, government forces targeted Indigenous communities with extreme genocidal violence, for which the then president, Rios Montt, was convicted in 2013, by the same brave High Risk Court. The verdict was overturned by the Constitutional Court soon after. Nevertheless, the Rios Montt trial created an important precedent for the possibility of justice for crimes against humanity and it generated confidence in the system. In addition, the ruling included the consideration of sexual violence against women as a tool of genocide and took women's cultural position as reproducers of community into account. The case laid the groundwork for the 2016 Sepur Zarco case.

While the case was successful in terms of conviction and procedure (see Burt 2019, Boesten 2022), the surviving women are still fighting for reparations. A dignified rollout of reparations requires a competent and willing government, which is problematic in many cases. However, with the help of national and international NGOs, these women work to keep the memory of what happened at Sepur Zarco alive – through testimonials and even plans for a comic book for children. These are difficult stories to tell, but commemorating the atrocities in a sensitive way could be transformative not only for the women and their families, but for Guatemala as a society, and indeed, for gender justice.

Sources: Boesten (2022) and Burt (2019)

to have their say. If we want to see what women's roles were during particular episodes of political violence, then we should look towards the arts. Poetry, music, and visual and performance art can often be more radical, accurate, and transformative in its depiction of women's experiences than 'official' commemorations. Similarly, women's experiences of non-political gender violence are often ignored and therefore politically denied. Creative activism is a powerful response, demanding accountability for violence, commemorating those who have lost their lives in these instances, and reminding society - its judges, lawyers, and police officers, politicians, policymakers, and journalists, as well as ordinary men and women - of the violent and unnecessary deaths of women and girls.

El Hogar Seguro, Guatemala

A group of feminist activist friends who were following the situation at the Hogar Seguro children's home in Guatemala on local television - from the girls' escape from the home to their detention and the fatal fire - decided to get together, determined not to let this be another forgotten tragedy in Guatemala's history. The group went straight to the morgue to support the affected families, and then organized themselves in a support group called Ocho Tijax (named after the tragedy's corresponding date on the Mayan calendar, with *tijax* - obsidian - representing a cut or a blade, or overwhelming division, pain, and separation). The girls were in the Hogar Seguro because of difficult situations at home or because they had run away or were vulnerable to trafficking; they were not criminals, but they were teenagers from poor socio-economic backgrounds and vulnerable in a violent and misogynist society. They were at this state institution supposedly for their own protection, but were met with further abuse, and even trafficking, according to the girls' claims. When they attempted to escape their situation, they were caught and eventually left to burn alive. A smear campaign accusing the girls and their families of criminal behaviour served to undermine any calls for justice coming from the children's families. Yet the solidarity of Ocho

Tijax, a group of professional women Mayra Jimenez, Quimy de León, Maria Peña, and Stef Arreaga, has allowed for a sustained campaign to keep the memory of the girls alive, and to pressure the state and the judiciary to take responsibility and seek justice.

Today, Ocho Tijax continues to accompany the families and the few survivors through medical and legal processes: they organize juridical counselling; physical and emotional healing therapy and psychology sessions for the survivors; and financial aid to cover transportation and other costs related to their campaigns for justice. In addition, and most visibly, they work to keep the children's memory alive. Ocho Tijax are affiliated with the media campaign NosDuelen56, which is organized by the families of the victims and focuses on demanding justice through the arts and journalism. The campaign exists to preserve and dignify the memory of the 56 teenage victims through collaborative cultural projects. Soon after the fire, NosDuelen56 built a memorial in Guatemala City's central square, Plaza de la Constitución, where relatives of the deceased gathered every Friday to honour the girls' memory and demand justice. In September 2019, the police removed the memorial, but it has since been replaced. Centrally located for everyone to see, the campaign is a powerful reminder of the state's responsibility and its neglect.

Another project NosDuelen56 carried out was a call to artists from all over the world to create portraits of the girls who died in the fire. In the campaign, 58 artists from Mexico, Italy, France, Spain, Argentina, and Guatemala participated and publicized the open call in their own countries. A follow-up call was made to invite more artists to join in creating images to support the campaign #NosDuelen56. One of the Guatemalan artists who participated was Sara Curruchich, an Indigenous Kaqchikel artist, composer, and singer who stressed the importance of the quest for justice:

> 'It's important to shine a light on the ways in which history and justice in Guatemala have been covered up, like the history of people suffering. This is happening yet again with the femicide of young girls. From our spaces [as artists] we demand justice, and we want to speak out for the girls - the survivors and those who died - who have left us with their strength to continue fighting for them.' (Rivera, 2017)

All this pressure has led to a judicial process against the director of the home and several other officials, but the process is littered with obstructions and delays and hearings have been continually postponed. Surviving relatives have faced mistreatment in court and those involved in the campaign, including the girls' families and their lawyers, have been intimidated and threatened. The Ocho Tijax collective itself has been intimidated, followed, and violently threatened, and is still receiving death threats today. Since the massacre in 2017, three relatives of the victims have been murdered - Gloria Pérez y Pérez, mother of Iris Yodenis León Pérez was killed in July 2018, alongside her 13-year-old daughter Nury León Pérez; María Elizabeth Ramírez, mother of Wendy Vividor Ramírez, was killed in February 2021. Recently, Elsa Sequín, another mother who works with Ocho Tijax and NosDuelen56, received death threats. Some activists involved with the campaign have fled the country for fear of retribution. As these activists emphasize in the podcast, considering the violence of the Guatemalan state and its disregard for and participation in violence against women and girls, keeping the memory alive through creative campaigns both inside and outside of Guatemala is extremely important.

Art, memory, and mobilization

Contemporary feminist art often places memory at its centre, as the podcast on Guatemala's Hogar Seguro case so clearly indicates. Remembering in the arts is more than recording events or experiences for posterity. Particularly in feminist art, memory often works as a reflection on the present - as a questioning, or perhaps a mirror of ongoing injustices. Artists such as Doris Salcedo (Bogotá, 1958), Natalia Iguiñiz (Lima, 1973), Lucila Quieto (Buenos Aires, 1977), and Claudia Martinez Garay (Ayacucho, 1983), draw on personal and collective memory to reflect on trauma, loss, and its aftershocks. In doing so, they also denounce the violence that caused the harm, allying their art to feminist activism. Apart from her more static photographic representations of the physical ruins of violence, Natalia Iguiñiz has also created arts-based research about a particular feminist activist brutally killed by political violence in 1992. In examining the life and work of María Elena Moyano, who was murdered and dynamited by Shining Path at a community event, Iguiñiz reflects on how Moyano was treated by political allies and enemies and offers a mirror to contemporary activists and politicians alike. Moyano's multiple identities as a feminist and political organizer and the intersecting factors of inequality that affected her as a Black woman of poor background made her life vulnerable as well as exemplary for so many others.[3] Indeed, in response to the question around what memorial art is, Amanda Jara, daughter of Chilean protest singer Víctor Jara says, 'It's looking at ourselves, and seeing where we've come from, what we've done - it's looking in the mirror' (Morris, 2017).

Figure 6.1: 'Independencia' from 'Buscando a María Elena', 2011. Credit: Natalia Iguiñiz

---

Box 6.2: Life and work of María Elena Moyano

María Elena Moyano was an Afro-Peruvian working-class woman, a political organizer in the United Left and a leader of women's organizations in her district. In the last years of her life, she was elected Deputy Mayor of Villa El Salvador, a self-built neighbourhood in the southern desert of Lima. Moyano mobilized the women in Villa to resist the violence of the State, Shining Path, and of their own husbands and boyfriends. She set up community kitchens to feed those in need and share the burden of care, she lobbied the local government for foodstuff and support, and she established alliances with middle-class feminists. She was also a clear target, and in her last visit to Villa while planning her escape to Spain, she was shot and dynamited in front of the community and in the presence of her children. The immediate political effect of her murder was a certain spread of fear and a weakening of the women's movement throughout the country, but she soon became a martyr of resistance. However, when the leadership of Shining Path was captured in the same year, 1992, Moyano's memory was co-opted.

As Jo-Marie Burt has argued (2011), Moyano's progressive and feminist politics were erased by opportunist political actors keen to capitalize on her widespread popular appeal. According to Burt, Moyano's memory was invoked in a Fujimorista discourse against Shining Path, as if she had supported the government and political movement led by dictator Alberto Fujimori 1990-2000. But Moyano had resisted the harassment and manipulation of the Fujimori government, recognized its abuses of human rights, and openly fought against its social and economic policies directed at her sector of society.

Besides the erasure of her left-wing politics and resistance to the Fujimori regime of the 1990s, through this co-optation, her feminism has hardly been remembered. The community care work of Maria Elena Moyano and her colleagues in women's organizations in Lima and throughout the country was political, as demonstrated through the responses of Shining Path – attempts at infiltration, defamation, threats, and even killings. Their work was also radical in its feminism: through their collective efforts, the women created vast networks of solidarity and learning that allowed women to defy patriarchal adversaries at home as well as on the streets. One of María Elena's colleagues who in 2018, when we spoke with her, still worked at the Casa de la Mujer – which they collectively set up in the 1990s – told us that it was María Elena who taught them about women's rights, and that learning about politics, including what we would now call gender politics or feminist politics, was very much part of their everyday engagement with the women's movement that María Elena had started in Villa El Salvador. Likewise, a young woman we met there, Carola, who works to encourage other young women in Villa to 'think politically', looked up to the memory of María Elena Moyano as her inspiration. So, when attending contemporary meetings at the Casa de la Mujer in Villa El Salvador, the community space originally established under María Elena's leadership, it is clear that her memory as a women's rights organizer is very much alive, and directly feeds into the contemporary struggles for women's rights and autonomy.

Natalia Iguiñiz, a visual artist based in Lima, studied her mother's archive for traces of María Elena. Iguiñiz's mother was a leftist activist in the 1980s and 1990s and had been friends with María Elena. Tracing this friendship through conversations, photographs, and letters, Iguiñiz made a series of portraits of Moyano that highlighted her feminism, her activism, her anger at injustice, and her joy in collective action. She then pasted a series of these portraits as posters on walls and columns in public spaces where contemporary Fujimoristas, including Moyano's own sister, had co-opted Moyano's memory for their own benefits. The resulting artwork, 'Buscando a María Elena' (Looking for María Elena, 2011), records a different memory of Moyano's life and her work; a memory that corresponds with the memory her friends have of her, and that captures what inspires contemporary and future generations.

Source: Boesten (2021)

The crossover between art and activism is often referred to as *artivism*. Those artists who explicitly use their art for political purposes, as in the case of much of Iguiñiz's work, are often themselves active in broader social mobilizations as well. For those themes and issues that are not considered on mainstream political agendas - such as women's rights and particular forms of political violence including the harassment of human rights defenders throughout the continent - creative forms of activism are a must. Arts including theatre, visual art, music, poetry, and dance tend to reach much wider and differentiated audiences than a street march can. Art is also a particularly powerful outlet for expressing historical trauma which is otherwise difficult to encompass, particularly those traumas that tend to be erased from formal commemorative practices. Thus, in the case of feminist activism in Latin America, the collective trauma of the infringement of basic human rights and continuous violence against women and the LGBTQ+ community in homes, public spaces, and in institutions, is increasingly mobilized in powerful manifestations of art and activism.

Box 6.3: Regina José Galindo

Regina José Galindo, born in 1974, is a performance artist and poet from Guatemala City. Regina harnesses art's emotive power to question histories of state violence and impunity and speak out on behalf of those affected. Her work often symbolically places her body in direct opposition to power, and under physical duress.

In one of her most famous performances *Quién puede borrar las huellas?* (Who Can Wipe Away the Footprints, 2003) she walked a bloody path from the Constitutional Court to the National Palace in Guatemala City, dipping her feet in human blood in memory of the Guatemalan armed conflict's victims and in rejection of the new presidential candidacy of General Efraín Ríos Montt who presided over some of the bloodiest years of the conflict. The performance won her the Golden Lion for Best Young Artist in the 51st Biennale of Venice (2005).

Regina states that her work is 'related to my context and my context is inevitably what happened with my history – so it's inevitable that all of my work has to do with death, impunity.' It formidably interrogates the pervasive trauma of Guatemala's national memory, creating combative and powerful symbols of resistance.

Speaking out in the face of extreme opposition is also the main theme in performance artist Regina José Galindo's piece *La Verdad* (The Truth). She sits centre stage reading aloud testimonies of the Indigenous Maya people who suffered massacre, torture, and rape at the hands of the Guatemalan military during the war. Many of them are witness statements by Maya Ixil women and have been taken from the April 2013 trial on genocide charges of Guatemala's former president, General Efraín Ríos Montt. Every 10 minutes, a dentist comes and injects Regina with anaesthetic, attempting to obstruct her speech. Over the course of the 60-minute performance, Regina's speech becomes increasingly muffled, but her words never cease.

Her work packs a visceral punch, embodying the difficulty and determination of speaking out in the face of injustice as well as becoming an homage to the memories of those affected, by repeating their stories. Actual testimony is central to the power of the piece, and Regina creates a striking physical metaphor of the Guatemalan state's attempt to silence victims of the war.

> 'My body was holding on with the purpose of demonstrating what I had learned about the strength of these women – because these women in the justice process of Rios Montt never faltered and the process was very long and torturous. In the end it was cancelled. The whole process was very conflicted, with every type of prevention, but these women continued with all of the force of the world.'

Regina's work has long focused on endemic violence in Guatemalan society, and in particular violence against women. Shortly after the murder of the 41 girls in the Hogar Virgen de la Asunción, José Galindo created an artistic response – *Las Escucharon Gritar y No Abieron La Puerta* (They Heard Them Screaming and They Didn't Open the Door). This was a sound performance in which 41 women were locked inside a small room shouting for nine minutes – the amount of time the girls at the Hogar Seguro spent screaming to be released while the classroom burned, before the police unlocked the door. Some of the mothers of the girls who died participated in the performance.

Stef Arrega of Ocho Tijax describes how the performance impacted her:

'For nine minutes the women screamed out with all their might, these screams came from the gut. This was something that as I talk about, it gives me goosebumps, just remembering that event. Because, outside the room where this artist was holding the performance, we had an exhibition of paintings, portraits of the girls who died, the 41 girls. So it was immensely emotional to be listening to those screams of horror inside that space, while the portraits of all those girls where there, present.'

Regina's process of artistic memory-making is designed to generate an impact within Guatemala and in the wider world about what happened, but it is also inherently personal, a way of making sense of the events for herself. Through it, she aims to 'close certain wounds – and understand what happened' in order to walk into the future.

Sources: Latin America Bureau (2022), Morris (2017)

Feminist artivism is associated with the use of bodies, music, words, and images in the public space to draw attention to gendered injustices on a societal scale. Arts are then used as a tool for conscientization (developing, strengthening, and changing consciousness), mobilization, and denunciation, and to disrupt the 'common sense' of everyday life in which even the most atrocious gendered harm is minimized, ignored, and denied. The families of the girls who died in the fire in the Hogar Seguro in Guatemala and the civil society organizations that support them actively use the arts to not only remember, but to mobilize and denounce; these are powerful acts of resistance that will remain, in the form of new memories and artefacts disseminated globally. As such, the arts - aided by social media platforms for dissemination - facilitate important transnational solidarity.

Those who feel threatened by these artivisms - the state, the military and their allies, particular groups of men, or conservatives - may try to take down the erected monuments as in Guatemala, or prohibit the plays or performances developed, as has happened in Peru, and even harass and threaten the activists, but this is increasingly counterproductive to their cause. Vianney Hernández, who lost her daughter in the fire in Hogar Seguro, understands very well that the government can destroy their memorial and obstruct the legal process, but it cannot erase her daughter's memory. Through continuous creative campaigns, Vianney and her colleagues keep the pressure up and keep their daughters' memory alive, as she discusses in the WRV podcast: 'The government wants to erase our children's memory and [I] can't allow it as a mother looking for justice'. Vianney inextricably links obtaining justice in the courts with preserving the girls' memory. Importantly, Vianney is surrounded by activists who will help her keep the memory alive, turning this initiative into an international campaign for justice in Guatemala.

Conclusion

Memorial arts, activist art, and feminist artivism are central to contemporary fights for social justice and women's and LGBTQ+ rights. The trauma of historical violence reverberates into the continuous everyday harm done to the bodies and lives of women, girls, and LGBTQ+ communities. Much contemporary feminist activism makes the link between historical trauma and continuous political and domestic violence. This connection between past, present, and future not only unsettles and rewrites understandings of the past and offers a mirror onto the present, but in doing so it also allows for a reimagining of the future. Guatemalan performance artist Regina José Galindo sees her memory work as essential for creating a better future for her daughter:

> 'Making memory in Guatemala, and not only in Guatemala but also in general, is necessary in order to become aware of the past, to manage the present and to have an idea of what kind of future can take shape. Especially when you have a daughter, you start to become aware that it is necessary to understand the past and to manage it.' (Morris, 2017)

Through artivism, individual trauma is turned into collective resistance, mobilization, and counter-memory. While not without danger - given multiple activists around Latin America report violence and intimidation in response to their work - it is potentially transformative; a powerful rethinking of how politics is done, who perpetuates violence against women and girls, who produces resistance, and who, what, and how society remembers and values.

Notes

1. See various statistics on violence against women in Guatemala at https://observatorio.mp.gob.gt/portal-estadistico.
2. The violence inflicted on Victoria Salazar, a Salvadorean migrant in Mexico, continued even after she was killed by police, through online reproductions and tabloid representations of her death. Tallulah Lines asks how we can contribute to mitigating violence against women and girls and avoid revictimizing women through the way we remember their deaths and their lives, for example, through murals dedicated to Salazar's life - and death - in Mexico city, in Lines (2021) 'Police brutally killed Victoria Salazar: how

are feminists representing her death in a dignified way?' at https://lab.org.uk/wrv-police-brutally-killed-victoria-salazar-how-are-feminists-representing-her-death-in-a-dignified-way.
3.   Drawing on Crenshaw's understanding of intersectionality (1991).

Bibliography

Boesten, J. (2022) 'Transformative gender justice: criminal proceedings for conflict-related sexual violence in Guatemala and Peru', *Australian Journal of Human Rights*, https://doi.org10.1080/1323238X.2021.2013701

Boesten, J. (2021) 'A feminist reading of sites of commemoration in Peru', in: Boesten, J. and H Scanlon, H. (eds.) *Gender, transitional justice and memorial arts: global perspectives on commemoration and mobilization.* Routledge Transitional Justice Series

Boesten, J. and Scanlon, H. (eds.) (2021) *Gender, transitional justice and memorial arts: global perspectives on commemoration and mobilization.* Routledge Transitional Justice Series

Burt, J.-M. (2011) 'Accounting for murder: the contested narratives of the life and death of María Elena Moyano', in: Bilbija, K. and Payne, L.A. (eds.) *Accounting for violence. Marketing memory in Latin America.* Durham and London: Duke University Press

Burt, J.-M. (2019) 'Gender justice in post-conflict Guatemala: the Sepur Zarco sexual violence and sexual slavery trial.' Critical Studies 4: 63-96.

Crenshaw, K. (1991) 'Mapping the margins: intersectionality, identity politics, and violence against women of color', *Stanford Law Review* 43(6), pp. 1241-1299

Latin America Bureau and King's College London (2022) 'Women Resisting Violence podcast', www.wrv.org.uk/podcast

Lugones, M. (2010) 'Toward a decolonial feminism', *Hypatia* 25(4), pp. 742-59

Morris, L. (2017) 'A call to art: memorial', *BBC Radio 4*, November, https://www.bbc.co.uk/programmes/b09dy204

Rivera, M. (2017) 'Nos duelen 56, una acción global por la justicia y por las niñas', https://prensacomunitar.medium.com/nos-duelen-56-una-acci%C3%B3n-global-por-la-justicia-y-porlas-ni%C3%B1as-ce60f7e3196c

Conclusion and recommendations

The most recent reports by international organizations on the intensification of violence against women and girls during the COVID-19 pandemic corroborate what women and women's organizations across Latin America have denounced for decades: that gendered and intersectional violence against them is both individual and structural and continues to have a devastating impact on their bodies, their communities, and their territories. These reports also confirm that violence against women because they are women has continued unabated (identified as a 'shadow pandemic' by UN Women), affecting them in their daily lives in private and public spaces.

Overall, the case studies presented in this book show compellingly the impact of the pandemic of violence against women and girls throughout the lifecycle, in multiple places and contexts, and the many forms that it takes. The pandemic of violence against women has raged across the continent, taking a huge toll on women and girls in rural and urban areas, and women from migrant and host communities. The pandemic of VAWG is experienced by women at home, in the workplace, in local markets, in forests, in mountains, and as they flee from conflict and poverty, seeking a way out of conflict and dispossession. Gendered and intersectional violence has also been perpetrated by state institutions and market actors against women human rights and land defenders during armed conflict, against Indigenous and Afro-descendant women in areas rich in natural resources, and against racialized women in urban peripheries.

The case studies portray a powerful narrative of protest and resistance. Despite legal achievements, which women and women's movements have contributed to, there is a low level of implementation and compliance with existing laws, compounded by widespread institutional and social impunity. Women's voices are loud and clear: gendered and intersectional violence is rampant in Latin America, and state and private institutions, including big businesses, have been weak to respond and even weaker - if not reluctant - to show accountability and enforce due diligence to ensure justice for crimes committed against women. These stories also bear witness to the weakness of the State in complying with international commitments (CEDAW, ILO) and enforcing existing legislation to ensure prevention of VAWG, protection of survivors, and punishment of perpetrators. In turn, the State itself and market actors emerge as major perpetrators of direct and indirect gendered violence throughout the continent. In the UK, policies toward migrants have had a negative impact on Latin American women as we saw in Chapter 5, but these women have organized and come together with other organizations to press for greater recognition of their needs.

One of the key messages resonating throughout the chain of women's voices is that gendered and intersectional violence against women and girls is the result of intersecting systems of oppression, namely heteronormative patriarchy, capitalism, colonialism, and racism. These overlapping power systems perpetuate women's structural subordination and further disenfranchise rural and urban Black, Indigenous, and migrant women, and trans people. They have also led to the high prevalence of femicides, especially of women leaders, as in the cases of Marielle Franco in Brazil and Berta Cáceres in Honduras (see Chapters 1 and 4).

Women have been standing up to gendered violence in mass mobilizations throughout the continent, such as in the #NiUnaMenos movement against femicide, and the pro-choice green wave that swept across Latin America demanding the de-criminalization of abortion. The chain of women's voices also denounces indifference and impunity surrounding sexual violence and the murders of women during armed and land conflicts (see Chapters 3 and 4). They tell us that in cases of militarized, institutional, and/or corporate-driven violence, women's resistance is fraught with danger. Nevertheless, up against the violent power of the State or *machista* violence inside their homes or in public places, it is often ordinary women who mobilize collectively to demand justice through courts, protests, and memorials. In addition to organizing resistance around textual and visual memorials through artivism, women are also using strategies which empower them to resist, mobilize, and denounce impunity. As Chapter 6 notes 'these are powerful acts of resistance that will remain in the form of new memories.' In this way, the arts, supported by social media, are a powerful tool for dissemination and facilitate international solidarity.

As important as women's capacity for political action through the arts is women's power for self and collective healing and for reconstructing their socio-political agency. As Chapter 5 discusses, Latin American migrant women 'have been at the forefront of developing artistic initiatives as therapy among survivors of gendered violence'. In addition, Latin American artists have also played a role in raising awareness and highlighting the plight of survivors, especially in light of the continuing taboo around many aspects of gender-based violence. Yet, it also shows that this must be accompanied by sustained campaigning and advocacy work to raise awareness and influence policymaking, as evidenced in the Step Up Migrant Women campaign in the UK.

Throughout the book, women's experiential knowledge emerges as a crucial element of resilience and agency. Women at the grassroots are building emancipatory knowledge, learning from their lived experiences of oppression and discrimination. In response to the overlapping power systems (patriarchy, racism, hetero-sexism) that reproduce extreme violence, women implement strategies for self-help and mutual support. A feminist intersectional ethics of care is one of the building blocks of the actions women undertake, individually and/or collectively, and shows women's power for transformation. Chapter 1 showed women's agency in building their own practices of resistance through individual short-term coping activities as well as longer-term collective initiatives that place a feminist ethics of care at their centre. The work of the community-based organization Casa das Mulheres in one of the poorest neighbourhoods of Rio de Janeiro to challenge and prevent gender-based violence, foster livelihoods, and provide support for women survivors of violence provides important insights into forms of resisting intersectional violence against women in cities.

In many compelling ways, the case studies engage us in a conversation on how women at the grassroots are implementing care strategies that are good for women, their communities, and nature. In Chapter 4, we learned that caring for nature and preserving environmental sustainability for future generations is part and parcel of women's visions for living well (*Buen Vivir*). In Chapter 2, we learned of the Care For Those Who Care regional campaign by domestic workers in response to labour abuse during the COVID-19 pandemic, which supported workers with practical advice and aimed to raise awareness among employers that domestic workers have labour rights.

These self-help practices are driven by values in direct opposition to capitalist visions of care as a commodity. The women's ethics of care also reclaims the rights of nature, and the obligation of states and businesses to respect and protect local ecosystems. This ethics of care is also decolonial, since it tackles the impact of racism and colonial power on the bodies and territories of rural, Indigenous, Afro-descendant, and Quilombola women. For this reason, reclaiming historically discarded ancestral knowledge is a key issue for women struggling at the grassroots. As Chapter 1 discusses, it is as crucial as creating emotional communities against intimate, economic, political, state, and institutional violence. Women's voices of resistance are critical of neoliberal policies and economic models that privilege market forces, big businesses, multinational companies, and economic elites. They are calling on their governments to implement human rights standards and regulations guaranteeing women's economic, social, and cultural rights as individuals and as members of collectives and peoples.

In Chapter 3, we saw how decades of sustained campaigning by the pro-choice women's movement led to debates throughout the continent and to the full legalization of abortion in some countries in the region. However, in a few others (namely El Salvador, Nicaragua, and Guatemala), the influence of the church has provoked a backlash against women's reproductive rights with more stringent measures and tougher penalties being introduced. In Chapter 4, we saw how women's organizations are emphasizing that violence against the land and territories is also violence done to their bodies, and its most palpable effects are in the denial of women's access to their sexual and reproductive rights, to land rights, and to a clean environment. All of these are key to ensure sustainable livelihoods for women, their families, and communities and also the conservation of nature, which is crucial for climate change preparedness.

Women's actions also demystify the socially constructed idea of women as victims of VAWG and demonstrate women's power for agency and social transformation. Transformation, they tell us, starts with oneself, as one becomes critically aware of unequal power relations and develops strategies and knowledge for self- and collective empowerment. This process galvanizes women's collective power to take action as women and as members of socially excluded peoples. Other examples of transformative changes given in the case studies are actions to make urban spaces safer for women through the *Safetipin* project in Bogota (see Chapter 1) which uses mobile apps to generate data on street lighting and public spaces, which are then used to influence public policy. We also learned of women-led initiatives and women's houses that are supporting women survivors of violence in communities throughout the region, leading to more structured initiatives to prevent violence and ultimately change public policies.

Several stories bear witness to the power of women at the grassroots to resist, counter, and neutralize the disempowering impact of gendered and intersectional violence in their daily lives. In Chapter 2, we learned that thanks to their advocacy and lobbying work, the extent of exploitation and discrimination endured by women domestic workers across private and public spaces has become better known to society and policymakers. We also learned of their efforts to influence the development of the finally adopted ILO Domestic Workers Convention 189. This is a landmark political achievement and women workers were key actors in its adoption. In line with domestic workers, rural and Indigenous women were key agents of change, by introducing new intersectional readings of CEDAW that could embrace the strategic needs and priorities of rural and Indigenous women (Chapter 4). All 20 Latin American countries have ratified the 1994 Inter-American Convention on the Prevention, Punishment and Eradication of Violence against Women (the Belém do Pará Convention), although most governments are not fulfilling their obligations under the treaty. Nevertheless, it is a useful advocacy tool for the women's movement, especially by the #NiUnaMenos campaign, which demands its effective implementation with budgets and public policies in place to stem the increasing levels of femicide and violence against women and girls.

Clearly, feminist and women's rights organizations, in alliance with social movements, have been critical agents of change in mobilizing forces and actions towards the eradication of all forms of VAWG. They have documented, exposed, and raised awareness of the everyday forms of violence women endure in their households, communities, and society at large. Their struggles have also exposed economic forms of VAWG that are often overlooked in official policy documents. This includes access to livelihoods, not being able to decide on the use of income that women earn themselves, or employers not paying domestic workers a decent wage. On a broader level, economic violence also means being dispossessed of rights to resources and assets like land and territory by the structural violence resulting from economic activities such as land grabbing and extractive mega-mining.

The central tenet of this book is that women at the grassroots are not only survivors of gender and intersectional violence but are also agents of social transformation and that their experiences are contributing in some cases to realizing gender equality and social justice. Their struggles are ongoing and target not only the drivers of violence in the household, within couples, at work, and in communities, but also the underlying structures that simultaneously produce and perpetuate those inequalities. A central claim is that women and girls in all their rich diversity are subjects entitled to rights (rights holders) and that any form of violence against them is a denial of their fundamental human rights.

Another important theme running through the book is the importance of listening to the chain of women's diverse voices from across and beyond the continent. In the LAB/King's College collaborative project, this was achieved through showcasing the Women

Resisting Violence blog and podcast. Although not all the chapters of the book are based on the WRV blog or podcast, these elements play an important role in the book as a whole. The podcast celebrates the innovative initiatives developed by women and shows how podcasting more generally can communicate and create hope and empathy. Indeed, in the voice of one of the participants in our final workshop on the role of podcasting to address VAWG and generate social transformation: 'Podcasting as a medium is very powerful because it generates intimacy with the listener... like whispering in their ear' (see Appendix).

Finally, the case studies presented in this book show the scale and breadth of VAWG in the region and map out women's relentless work to overcome its harmful impacts. The case studies also demonstrate how women at the grassroots are leading the way in this struggle for social justice and that these actions and strategies deserve upscaling into higher levels of policymaking. Their message is that policymakers need to engage in transformative processes of policymaking to eradicate gendered and intersectional VAWG. In practice, this means designing and implementing policies that address the underlying factors that (re)produce gendered and intersectional violence against women and girls, and give less priority to market shifts and business activities that privilege elitist capital accumulation at whatever cost (including nature's depletion). The following points represent some concrete actions stemming from women's strategic experiences that policymakers could consider adopting that will strengthen laws and policies for eradicating gender and intersectional inequalities:

Policy recommendation 1: Policy and legal narratives need to address VAWG as a violation of human rights and enforce equality and non-discrimination as legally binding obligations (following the Belem do Pará Convention on the prevention, punishment, and eradication of all forms of violence against women and Sustainable Development Goal [SDG] 5 Target 5.2).

Policy recommendation 2: Policy and legal narratives need to address 'access to sexual and reproductive health and rights' (SDG 5, target 5.6) as a serious human right and binding obligation.

Policy recommendation 3: Listen to and believe women's testimonies of VAWG and use their narratives as reliable data to inform policies and legislation.

Policy recommendation 4: Develop nationwide programmes for justice providers (judges, policy, forensic staff, and others) on frameworks relevant to women's right to a life free from violence. Include raising critical awareness of social norms and gender-based and intersectional discrimination and inequalities.

Policy recommendation 5: Develop national school curricula that include gender awareness, equality, and history from the perspective of colonized and enslaved peoples.

Policy recommendation 6: Increase funding and other resources for women's refuges and to support women survivors of violence (counselling, health care, legal aid, and income generation).

Policy recommendation 7: Hold to account States that condone and/or ignore VAWG and especially femicides and extractivist GBV, through regional and international policy processes (such as the Belem do Pará Convention) via national legislation and the Inter-American Commission on Human Rights.

Policy recommendation 8: In order to better address intersectional violence and discrimination and to ensure inclusive policies, it is essential that disaggregated data be collected at local and regional levels to address the situation of all women (according to race, ethnicity, age, sexual orientation etc.).

Policy recommendation 9: States and civil society should learn from and listen to existing campaigning/advocacy and grassroots initiatives to address VAWG and fund mechanisms to capture innovative collective resistance strategies.

Policy recommendation 10: Alternative forms of visibilizing the experiences of VAWG and women's resistance should be given greater prominence and used more effectively to influence policy. These include various forms of arts-based and memorializing initiatives, including the role of podcasts which are foregrounded and celebrated here.

***

The WRV Collective

Appendix: Women Resisting Violence, the multilingual podcast

Background and context

A core element of the Women Resisting Violence project has been a podcast comprising three episodes focusing on women in Brazil, Guatemala, and the UK; it also includes a bonus episode from a workshop on 'Listening to Women Resisting Violence', all of which are hosted on our WRV/Latin America Bureau dedicated website. Several of the chapters in the book draw heavily on interviews that informed the podcast; others depended on topics and interviews that were not included in the series.

Podcasts can provide an interesting platform for facilitating listening and ensuring that diverse voices are heard. The WRV podcast was designed to foreground the voices of women who have developed a range of transformative resistance practices, initiatives, and campaigns to address and mitigate VAWG. It spotlights the experiences of women survivors alongside examples of innovative projects and campaigns to mitigate gendered and intersectional violence. A collaborative production, the podcast aimed to develop meaningful conversations around resisting VAWG and to share and exchange first-hand knowledge of addressing VAWG internationally. As well as recounting stories of resistance, the podcast was itself conceived as a tool to engender resistance by amplifying women's political and social agency. Podcasts are an engaging format to ensure that their voices are heard, building empathy for their experiences through the intimacy of listening.

The WRV series is partly inspired by the work of US-based Radio Ambulante, a narrative podcast telling Latin American stories in Spanish, with an accompanying English transcript. It was also inspired by the rise of multilingual podcasting, which recognizes that many of us make sense of the world in more than one language. While the series aimed to share knowledge and highlight the voices of women resisting violence in various ways, the episodes were not created by the women themselves as a form of community broadcasting. Instead, the focus was on creating highly produced stories that captured the women's experiences and aimed to reach as wide an audience as possible. This was further facilitated by translating and dubbing the episodes in at least two languages (among English, Spanish, and Portuguese). It was especially important to us that the episodes were accessible to the organizations featured and that you could hear their stories told in their own languages.

In terms of substance and production, the podcast draws on our collective research (McIlwaine and Boesten), policy (Thomson and Muñoz Cabrera), audio production (Morris), and writing and editing (Wilson) experience in Latin America and beyond, as a collaboration between King's College London and the Latin America Bureau. It also involved a range of other collaborators including Renata Peppl as the presenter of the series, sound engineer Eliane Correa, Janno Media who produced the fourth bonus episode, LAB contributors who translated the recordings, and non-professional dubbing artists (see below for a complete list).

The episodes

The first episode, **Mourning the 56 in Guatemala**, focuses on the work of Ocho Tijax, a women's collective established in the wake of a tragedy on 8 March 2017 when 56 girls were locked in a classroom of their state-run children's home just outside Guatemala City, after trying to run away. When a fire broke out, only 15 survived. Five years later no one has been sentenced for these crimes. Ocho Tijax cares for the girls' families and the survivors as well as fighting their case in the courts. The episode also includes a conversation with Vianney, the mother of Ashly Angelie Rodriguez Hernández, who lost her life in the fire. This is available in English and Spanish, with a Portuguese transcript on our website.

The second episode, **Rio's Trailblazing Women's House**, tells the story of the Casa Das Mulheres, part of the NGO, Redes da Maré run by Eliana Sousa Silva and her colleagues in the favelas of Maré in Rio de Janeiro. Casa das Mulheres, coordinated by Julia Leal, provides education around gender violence and support for those leaving abusive relationships, in an area where the police refuse to intervene, together with a range of livelihoods and arts projects. It has also been a lifeline for many during COVID when many favela residents lost their jobs, providing work, making masks, and distributing food to starving families – as well as dealing with a huge rise in domestic violence. This is available in English and Portuguese, with a Spanish transcript on our website.

The third episode, **Step Up Migrant Women**, focuses on the experiences of women resisting gendered violence in the UK. It includes Gil's story of migrating to the UK from Brazil with her partner and children as a tourist, and subsequently becoming undocumented. When Gil fled abuse, she was met with hostility by UK police and ended up homeless with a child in mid-December. Finding the Latin American Women's Rights Service (LAWRS) changed her life and Gil now works on the group's Step Up Migrant Women campaign, coordinated by Elizabeth Jiménez-Yáñez, to highlight the vulnerability of migrant women with insecure immigration status in situations of domestic abuse. LAWRS also works with Migrants in Action (MinA), led by Carolina Cal Angrisani, a community theatre group dedicated to Brazilian women in London who have experienced gender-based violence. Through theatre and the arts, they build a sense of community, understand and break cycles of violence and raise their visibility as migrant women. This is available in English, Spanish, and Portuguese.

The bonus episode, **Listening to Women Resisting Violence**, is produced by Janno media and based on an online discussion around the power of podcasting for social change. This episode contextualizes the compelling stories of transformation and solidarity showcased in the Women Resisting Violence podcast. Thanks to all who contributed to this discussion, including leading audio producers from Latin America, representatives from the fearless women's organizations featured in the podcast, women who dubbed their voices in the podcast, and a wider public of organizations, activists, social workers, and students. This episode is available in English.

The process

Led by the producer, Louise Morris, the podcasts' narratives centred on interviews with key participants who recounted their experiences of resisting gendered violence individually or collectively. Due to geographical distance and the pandemic, most of the interviews were conducted remotely, with the exception of two in the UK. Alongside Louise, an additional interviewer/translator supported the recordings. Questions were agreed by the team in advance and usually asked in the mother tongue of the interviewee, to ensure they felt as comfortable as possible. Louise then worked with transcripts translated by LAB contributors, to cut down the hours of interview material and weave the conversations into a compelling narrative to illuminate the women's projects, campaigns, and lived experiences. She then cut the audio into this structure in the three language versions, adding sound design, atmosphere, and music to draw the listener into the stories and add context, and wrote links to thread the interviews together.

New transcripts and translations of the episodes were made by LAB contributors in order to dub the interviews.

Some of the interviewees provided their own dubbing in their second language; in cases where this was not possible, dubbing actors were used. We worked with non-professional dubbing artists from the same regions as the contributors and with a direct connection to the issues discussed, to convey the sentiments of the interviewees authentically across all language versions. Finally, the links were recorded by our presenter Renata Peppl in all three languages, and Louise edited and placed these and the dubs in the various language versions – seven episodes in total. Finally, Louise mastered each episode, enhancing the audio and adjusting levels to the specifications of podcast platforms and uploaded them for distribution.

Music was provided by Rebeca Lane, a Guatemalan hip-hop artist, musicians from the Maré favelas, and WARA, whose music tackles the experiences of Latin American migrants in the UK.

Reflections on the podcast process

A number of key issues arose from the final workshop that included several key podcast producers from Latin America.

- The podcast is a means to listen to those affected by violence, a means to denounce that violence, and a way to remember and record that memory for the future.
- Podcasts empower in their ability to inform women in the specific context of the podcast, as well as to allow these women to speak to wider audiences.
- Podcasts can be a means to affirm and grow communities by making links and sharing with other communities, to further collective action.
- Podcasts give visibility to the everyday battles of women resisting violence, locally and transnationally.
- Podcasts create an intimacy between speaker and listener that improves communication between victim-survivors as well as between affected communities and wider audiences.
- Listening to those most affected is essential if we are to change the political structures and discriminatory practices which impinge on women's daily lives and (re)produce gender and social norms that subordinate women and girls and uphold violence and impunity.

Of course, podcasting is not without its shortcomings. Indeed, podcast production is not always accessible to women's grassroots organizations, as making highly produced podcasts requires technical expertise, access to expensive equipment, resources, interpreters, and so on. In some contexts, radio may be a more popular medium for sharing stories and information at the grassroots level. However, this isn't the only way to make podcasts, as free apps and decent microphones on mobile phones now make recording and sharing audio digitally ever more accessible. Production companies like South Africa-based Volume are using voice notes on WhatsApp as a new method for distributing podcasts. Given that organizations like Redes da Maré regularly use voice notes on WhatsApp to communicate and record their voices, there is potential for podcasts to make major inroads as a popular form of knowledge transfer among the marginalized moving forward. In fact, Latin America is the fastest growing region for podcast consumption (Grand Review Research, 2021).

As Stef Arreaga of Ocho Tijax attested in the workshop, 'The podcast is an act of remembrance and it's a historical document.' For Gil Garcia, contributing to the podcast marked 'a breakthrough from being a survivor to being a voice for the community.' Ana Rojas, who dubbed Gil's voice highlighted how 'this podcast internationalizes the fight of women'. For Mexican podcast producer Diego Morales, podcasting is 'a way of communicating, of building hope'. For Carolina Cal of MinA Theatre,

> 'the podcast connected our work with other organizations in and out of the UK. It has put MinA's work in wider context, bringing visibility to the issues involving Brazilian women in the UK and raising the question of how we can use the arts to personally and collectively heal, empower our community, and fight the system.'

The podcast was shortlisted for Best Documentary in the Amnesty International Media Awards 2022.

People involved in creating the podcasts

Women Resisting Violence is presented by Renata Peppl and produced by Louise Morris, with research and assistance from Cathy McIlwaine, Jelke Boesten, Marilyn Thomson, Patricia Muñoz Cabrera, Moniza Rizzini Ansari, Noelle Resende, and Rebecca Wilson. Featuring the stories of Vianney Claret Hernandez Mejia, Stef Arreaga, Mayra Jimenez, Quimy de León, Carolina Cal, Gil Garcia, Elizabeth Jimenez-Yañez, Eliana Sousa Silva, Julia Leal, and Michele Gandra. Made through a partnership with King's College London and the Latin America Bureau. Additional recording engineering from Eliane Correa and Ameno Cordóva. Translation by Cristina Reynoso López, Natasha Tinsley, Hebe Powell, Ella Barnes, Luciana Lopes, Jennifer Alexander, Morgan Fairless Brown, and Theodora Bradford. Dubbing from Cecilia Cruz, Alma Carballo, Esmeralda Lobos, Larisa Muñoz, Juliana Postico, Claudia Alves, Giselle Nirenberg, Ana Lucía Rojas, Mariana Reyes, and Najlla Kay. Featuring music by Rebeca Lane, WARA, Jonathan Panta, Rafael Rocha, Serena Assumpção, Gilberto Martins, and Uppbeat.

Bibliography

Grand View Research (2021), 'Podcasting market size, share & trends analysis report by genre (news & politics, society & culture, comedy, sports), by format (interviews, panels, solo, conversational), by region, and segment forecasts, 2021-2028', https://www.grandview research.com/industry-analysis/podcast-market

Index

Page numbers in *italics* refer to figures, those in **bold** indicate boxes.